AGGRESSORS

VOLUME 4

PATROL AIRCRAFT VS. SUBMARINE

Text by Dr. ALFRED PRICE

Illustrations by RIKYU WATANABE

U.S. Navy Avengers and a subchaser (PC-551) in joint air-sea ASW exercises off Miami, Florida in March 1943. (National Archives)

Front of jacket: Consolidated Liberator GR VI anti-submarine aircraft, Type XXI and Type VIIC/41 U-boats.

Frontispiece: Type 0 Mk 11 Observation Seaplane (F1M2) and USS *Torsk* (SS-423) (Norio Hirano, National Archives)

Copyright © by Zokeisha Publications Ltd., Tokyo/New York. All rights reserved.
Edited by Yoji Watanabe.

First published in the United States of America by Howell Press, Inc.,
700 Harris Street, Suite B, Charlottesville, Virginia 22901.
Telephone (804) 977-4006.

Library of Congress Catalog Card Number 89-82171
ISBN 0-943231-37-X
Printed in Japan.
First Printing
HOWELL PRESS

*All "miles" given are "nautical miles."

Introduction

Maritime warfare during the twentieth century has been dominated by the rise of two new weapon systems: the aircraft and the submarine. Great is the contrast between them. The aircraft: fast, brash, noisy, all-seeing and in the open for all to see, at the same time both fragile and vicious. The submarine: slow, stealthy, silently stalking its prey and delivering its blow, then slipping back into the depths to make its escape.

The most intensive phase of operations between aircraft and submarines took place during the six years of World War II. At the start of that conflict aircraft posed little threat to well-handled submarines: they lacked the radius of operation necessary to reach sea areas far from land; they lacked the detection and location equipment necessary to find submarines in poor visibility or beneath the surface; they lacked weapons that were effective against those submarines they did find; and they were available in numbers insufficient to impose any great pressure on the enemy. Moreover there was little reliable Intelligence on the whereabouts of enemy submarines, so the few maritime patrol aircraft available wasted much of their time scouring sea areas where there were no ene-my submarines to be found.

During World War II the German U-boats came close to severing the maritime artery between the USA and Great Britain, and had they succeeded, the latter nation might have been starved into submission and an invasion of continental Europe rendered out of the question. The U-boat menace had to be defeated, and neither effort nor wealth was spared in the attempt. By 1945 scientists and technicians in Great Britain and the USA, working in close cooperation, had developed the maritime patrol aircraft to the point where it posed a potent threat to enemy submarines attempting to operate in the Atlantic and Pacific theaters. Each deficiency limiting the effectiveness of such aircraft at the beginning of the war had been made good: they now had the range to cover shipping wherever they needed to go; they carried electronic detection and location systems to pinpoint the position of submarines; they had weapons that were effective against submarines on the surface or submerged; they were available in numbers sufficient to impose enormous pressure on the submariners; and those directing the aircraft into action had the necessary Intelligence information to send them where they would be most effective. This book tells the story of the evolutionary changes that brought this about.

U848 (Type IXD₂) attacked by Consolidated PB4Y patrol bombers of VB-107, southeast of Ascension Island in the South Atlantic on 5 November 1943. (National Archives)

A Lockheed Hudson I of No. 206 Squadron, Coastal Command, on patrol over Heligoland Island. (Imperial War Museum)

Forging the Weapon

When the Second World War opened in Europe in September 1939, Royal Air Force Coastal Command's maritime patrol force was the largest and most effective possessed by any of the belligerent nations. Yet it comprised only ten squadrons of Avro Anson patrol aircraft with limited range, one squadron of Lockheed Hudsons not yet ready for action, two of Short Sunderlands, and four squadrons with obsolete biplane flying boats. Of these types only the Hudson and the Sunderland could be considered as up-to-date, and moves were under way to reequip most of the force with these aircraft. Also at this time the Royal Navy possessed six aircraft carriers with some 150 single-engined Fairey Swordfish and Blackburn Skua aircraft able to perform the maritime patrol role. As yet none of these aircraft was fitted with radar, though in Britain the first airborne sets were undergoing trials.

At the outbreak of war the Sunderland flying boat was the most effective long range maritime patrol aircraft in service in any of the belligerent nations. With a maximum take-off weight of 20 tons, this aircraft could carry a 2,000 lb (907 kg) bomb load and was able to spend up to two hours on patrol 600 miles (1,110 km) from base. Beyond that distance from sheltered bays from which flying boats could operate, the U-boats were safe from air attack unless one of the few Royal Navy aircraft carriers happened to be in its area.

The Sunderland crews had only their eyesight, assisted by binoculars, with which to find enemy submarines. The first primitive airborne radars for installation in patrol aircraft were undergoing trials, but no aircraft in service at this time carried such equipment. No aircraft carried equipment to detect or locate submarines beneath the surface. Thus in conditions of poor visibility, or at night, or if they were submerged in any but the clearest of waters, the boats were almost immune from detection.

To attack those enemy submarines they did find, the Sunderlands carried thin-cased anti-submarine bombs weighing 100 lb (45 kg), 250, or 500 lb (113, or 227 kg). The explosive power of these weapons would have been adequate to sink or disable an enemy boat, but only if they detonated close to it. To achieve this the fuse fitted to the bombs was one of the most complex in existence at the time: after the bomb left the aircraft, the rotation of a small vane on the nose through a certain number of turns made the bomb "live;" if it then struck anything hard (i.e., a submarine or surface vessel) the fuse would set off the main charge; if the bomb struck the surface of the sea, the lesser shock started a previously-set timing mechanism to allow the bomb to sink to a depth of about 50 ft (15 m) and detonate there. In operation it was found that the fuses fitted to the anti-submarine bombs were liable to leak water which prevented them from working.

There were other problems with the anti-submarine bombs, as the crew of an Anson of No. 233 Squadron discov-

Four 250 lb (113 kg) anti-submarine bombs hung on racks inside a Short Sunderland. (Imperial War Museum)

A Focke-Wulf Fw200C-3 long-range KG (*Kampfgeschwader*) 40 takes off for shipping search. (Bundesarchiv)

Blohm und Voss BV138C during the attack with depth charges off the Norwegian coast. (Bundesarchiv)

ered on 5 September 1939, just two days after the outbreak of the war. On patrol off the west of Scotland, the aircraft surprised a submarine on the surface and released a couple of 100-pounders (45 kg bombs) on the boat as it was submerging. The bombs, dropped from low altitude, struck the sea at a shallow angle and skipped back into the air like a couple of flat stones. The impact initiated their time fuses, however, and after a short pause both bombs detonated in the air beneath the Anson. The splinters from the bombs caused severe damage to the aircraft, which forced the crew to ditch; they boarded their dinghy and were rescued soon afterwards. Only later did the scale of the fiasco become clear: the submarine involved was the Royal Navy boat HMS *Seahorse*, and the only damage to her occurred when she struck the bottom in the haste to dive to safety!

Compounding all of these deficiencies was the lack of adequate Intelligence on the whereabouts of enemy submarines, which meant that maritime patrol aircraft wasted most of their limited time scouring areas in which there were no enemy submarines anyway.

Yet for all its limited capability, at the outbreak of war the combined force of maritime patrol aircraft operated by the Royal Air Force and the Royal Navy was superior to those of any of the other nations involved in the conflict. The French Navy operated a hodge-podge collection of obsolescent flying boats for oversea reconnaissance. The German *Luftwaffe* operated a mixed bag of modern and obsolete landplanes and flying boats in this role, but its anti-submarine patrol operations were confined to the Baltic and the waters off northwest Germany.

The Submarine in 1939

When the war began only the German Navy operated submarines against enemy sea traffic in the commerce-raiding role. At the outbreak of war, that force had 56 U-boats in commission, 46 of which were ready for action but only 22 of which were of the ocean-going 750-ton Type VII version. On the surface the Type VII had a maximum speed of 17 knots and a maximum range of 6,500 miles (12,040 km) at 12 knots; running submerged on limited battery power, its maximum speed was 8

Two Type VII U-boats tie up at a port in Norway. (Bundesarchiv)

The Short Sunderland Mk I of No. 210 Squadron on convoy duty over the Atlantic. (Imperial War Museum)

knots, or it could cover 72 miles (133 km) at 4 knots. The boat's armament comprised five torpedo tubes and a single deck-mounted 88 mm gun, and rifle-caliber machine guns could be fired from the conning tower. When it encountered enemy aircraft the main defense was to submerge, which took a Type VII about 50 seconds.

Because of their limited underwater speed and range, the U-boats spent most of their time on the surface, submerging only when they needed to avoid being seen by the enemy. Thus the term "submarine" was something of a misnomer: "submersible boat" describes their capabilities more accurately.

From personal experience Admiral Karl Dönitz, commander of the German U-boat force, knew that a single boat had little chance of mounting an effective attack on an escorted convoy (as a U-boat commander in World War I, his attempt to do so ended with the loss of the boat and his spending the rest of the war in British captivity). To overcome this problem the German commander devised the "Wolf Pack" tactic for U-boats operating against escorted convoys. The boats were to operate not in ones or twos, but in fives, tens, or even more. Such a force operating against Atlantic convoys would set up a patrol line running north-south, with individual boats 20 miles (37 km) apart, and wait for an Allied convoy to fall into the trap. As soon as the lookouts on one of the U-boats sighted the convoy, that boat made no attempt to attack but instead fell into position behind the enemy ships, remaining on the surface, and broadcast to headquarters regular radio reports on its position and heading. Remaining on the surface, the other boats in the pack converged on a position ahead of the enemy ships, and when the convoy arrived at that point, they launched a concerted attack from several directions.

The defeat of France in the spring of 1940 provided the German Navy with valuable bases on the Bay of Biscay leading out into the Atlantic: Bordeaux, La Pallice, St. Nazaire, Lorient, and Brest. By the end of the first year of the war, the U-boat fleet had expanded considerably, and Admiral Dönitz now had sufficient submarines to bring into play the "Wolf Pack" tactic. The effectiveness of these methods was conclusively demonstrated in October 1940 when, during the nights of 17/18 and 19/20, U-boats attacked the eastbound convoys HX79 and SC7, sinking 33 ships and damaging three others. For the German submariners, these were "The Happy Times."

Despite their limited ability to find and destroy enemy submarines, there was a great deal patrol aircraft could do to nullify these tactics, and the presence of even a single aircraft in the vicinity of a convoy gave considerable protection from attack. An aircraft sweeping the area ahead of the convoy might force the boats in the German patrol line to dive, providing the convoy with a good chance of passing through the pack without being sighted. If the shadowing U-boat was forced to dive, it could not broadcast position reports and would soon lose contact with the convoy. Then a sharp turn might take the ships safely out of the trap laid for them. Thus the "Wolf Pack" tactics were extremely vulnerable to interference from the air and were rarely successful when patrol aircraft were present. However, it did not take long for the German Navy high command to learn of the existence of the so-called "Atlantic Gap"—the area in the mid-Atlantic bounded by arcs of radius 600 miles (1,110 km) from the Allied air bases in Newfoundland, Iceland, and Northern Ireland. The Royal Air Force maritime patrol aircraft could not reach that area of ocean, leaving the U-boats free to practice their Wolf Pack tactics with impunity. Because of this, the Atlantic Gap became a veritable graveyard for Allied shipping during the first three years of the war.

The Introduction of Radar and New Weapons

From the beginning of the war, Royal Air Force Coastal Command had pressed hard to get radars for its aircraft, and in January 1940 12 Hudsons were issued to Nos. 220, 224, and 233 Squadrons fitted with the ASV (Air to Surface Vessel) Mark I radar developed at the Telecommunications Research Establishment at Swanage. The set operated on a frequency of 214 Megahertz, and fixed aerials fitted to the nose searched the sea only in front of the aircraft. During trial flights against a British submarine, the radar located the boat on the surface at $5\frac{1}{2}$ miles (10.2 km) from 3,000 ft (910 m), but at that altitude the submarine was lost in "sea clutter" at ranges below $4\frac{1}{2}$ miles (8.3 km). A far more effective altitude for a radar search was found to be 200 ft (60 m), where the submarine was seen at $3\frac{1}{2}$ miles (6.5 km) and observed down to $\frac{1}{2}$ mile (930 m) before it disappeared in sea clutter. The radar had been carefully set up for the trial, however, and those carried by operational aircraft rarely gave this level of performance and their general reliability was poor. Coastal Command crews found ASV I barely effective as a means of locating submarines. It was useful in assisting them to rendezvous in poor visibility with the convoys they were to escort (large ships could be seen at ranges up to 12 miles (22.2 km) and for general navigation (coastlines could be seen from 20 miles (37 km or more.).

The main contribution of ASV Mark I was that it demonstrated the operational value of radar for maritime patrol aircraft, if the equipment could be given better performance and greater reliability. The upshot was that a redesigned and greatly improved set, the ASV Mark II, appeared in the spring of 1940. The Mark II operated on 176 Megahertz and had a more powerful transmitter, a more sensitive receiver, and was considerably more reliable than its predecessor. Moreover, technicians at Swanage developed a sideways-looking aerial array which greatly improved the detection range of ASV. The array was fitted to a Whitley bomber and comprised eight transmitter aerials arranged in an oblong along each side of the rear fuselage and four posts, extending four feet (1.2 m) above the rear fuselage, each carrying two receiver aerials. The large array focused the transmitter power into a narrow beam extending sideways from the aircraft, switched rapidly between the two sides. Tests demonstrated the value of the new array: with the aircraft flying at 2,000 ft (610 m), a surfaced submarine was observed at 20 miles (37 km) when it was side-on and at 12 miles (22 km) when it was bows-on; sea clutter concealed the boat at ranges less than 5 miles (9.3 km). When the Whitley flew at 1,000 ft (300 m), the ranges were 10 miles, 7 miles, and 3 miles (19 km, 13 km, and 5.6 km) respectively. The Royal Air Force placed an order for 4,000 ASV Mark II sets, but due to the even more pressing need for radar for the air defense of Great Britain, it would be well into 1941 before the new ASV was available in quantity.

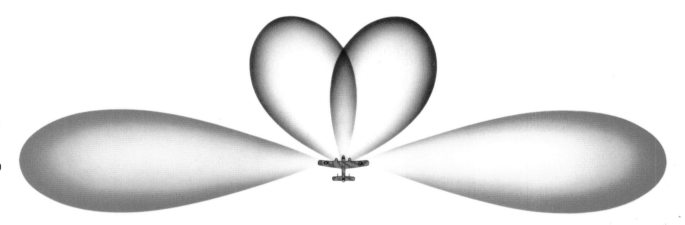

Radar coverage of ASV Mk II on Whitley bomber

The radar operator could select either the forwards or the sideways-looking antennas, but not both at the time. The normal method of search was to use the sideways-looking antennas, which enabled the operator to cover a 24-mile (44 km) wide strip of water; when contact was made, the aircraft would turn through 90 degrees towards it, and home-in using the forward-looking antennas.

Armstrong Whitworth Whitley Mk VII fitted with ASV Mk II radar antennas on the fuselage, under the wing and nose. (Imperial War Museum)

Leigh Light installed on a Coastal Command Liberator. (Imperial War Museum)

With the new ASV Mark II radar, it was possible to detect enemy submarines on the surface at night at a reasonable range. But if the aircraft turned towards it to make an attack, at about one mile (1.9 km) from the boat, its echo signals merged into the "sea clutter" making it impossible to conduct an accurate attack using radar alone. What was needed was a method of bridging the final mile to the target. Aircraft had conducted experiments in an attempt to illuminate the submarine with the low-intensity flares then available, but these offered little hope of success against a target liable to disappear within half a minute of any such warning. With this in mind Squadron Leader Humphrey Leigh secured official backing to fit a Naval 24 in (61 cm) searchlight on a retractable mounting in the position originally occupied by the ventral gun turret of the Wellington bomber. The searchlight put out an intense but narrow beam, which under Leigh's system could be trained on the submarine and held there by an operator in the nose of the aircraft. Full scale trials in the spring of 1941 using a search-light-fitted Wellington and a Royal Navy submarine demonstrated that the Leigh Light, as it became known, was feasible, though a great deal of time and effort would be needed to perfect the system, put it into production, and train operational crews to use it effectively.

The use of the Royal Air Force anti-submarine bombs in action had demonstrated that the weapon was far more dangerous to the user and rather less dangerous to the enemy than had been hoped. However, even if the program had top priority, it would take about two years to develop a new weapon from scratch. And in the meantime Coastal Command had a life and death battle to fight. The only other weapon suitable for use against submarines that was available in Britain was the drum-shaped naval 450 lb (204 kg) depth charge, a well-proven device which had been in service with few changes since 1918. Trials with the weapon showed that if dropped from the air it would detonate satisfactorily, provided the aircraft was not flying too fast or too high at the time of release. By the late spring of 1940, these trials spawned a makeshift weapon for use by anti-submarine aircraft: a standard naval depth charge, with a rounded fairing on one end and fins on the other to stabilize its passage through the air.

The modified naval depth charge promised three major advantages over the anti-submarine bombs it was to replace. First, the well-proven hydrostatic pistol was far more reliable than the complex fuse fitted to the bomb. Secondly, nearly three-quarters of the weight of the weapon was high explosive, compared with only half in the case of the anti-submarine bomb. And thirdly, the hydrostatic pistol would detonate the weapon only when it reached a previously set water pressure, and there was no risk of it bouncing off the water and detonating in the air. The 450 lb (204 kg) depth charge quickly replaced the 500 lb (227 kg) anti-submarine bomb; later a 250 lb (113 kg) depth charge was developed to replace the smaller anti-submarine bombs.

The depth charges were a major improvement over the weapons they replaced, but still all too few attacks on subma-

The Fairey Albacore with two 450 lb (204 kg) depth charges lands aboard HMS *Illustrious*. (Imperial War Museum)

Section at control room and tower of Japanese Navy *Kaidai* 7 class submarine (*I-176–I-185*)

Displacement
Surfaced: 1,833 tons
Submerged: 2,602 tons
Dimensions
Length: 105.5 m (346 ft 1 $^{11}/_{16}$ in)
Beam: 8.25 m (27 ft $^{13}/_{16}$ in)
Draught: 4.6 m (15 ft 1 $^{1}/_{8}$ in)
Propulsion
Diesel engines: 2 × 4,000 hp
Electric motors: 2 × 900 hp
Max speed
Surfaced: 23.1 knots (42.8 km/h)
Submerged: 8 knots (14.8 km/h)
Range
Surfaced: 8,000 nautical miles (14,820 km)
 at 16 knots (29.6 km/h)
Submerged: 50 nautical miles (93 km)
 at 5 knots (9.3 km/h)
Safety operation depth
80 m (260 ft)
Armament
Bow torpedo tubes: 6
1 × 12 cm (4.7 in) gun
2 × twin 25 mm cannon
Crew 86

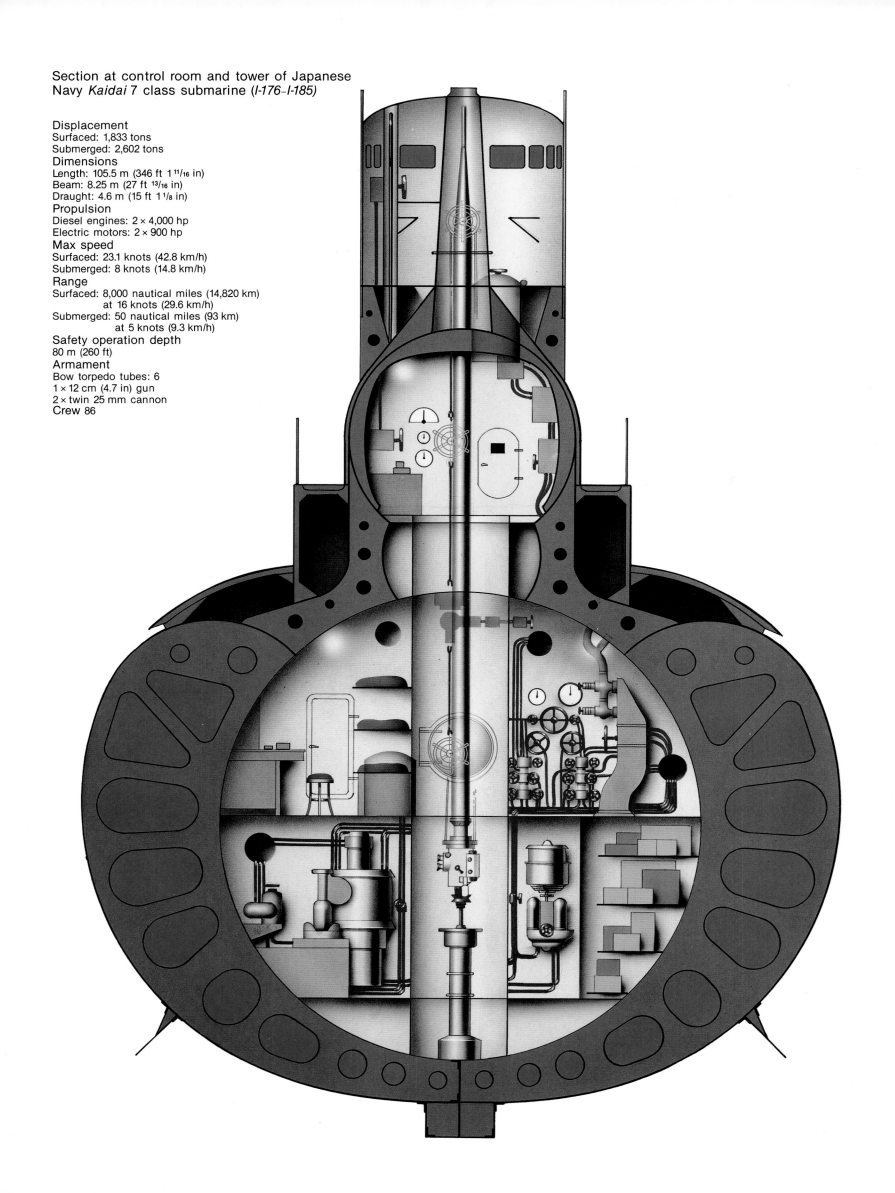

Type VIIC U-boat Cutaway

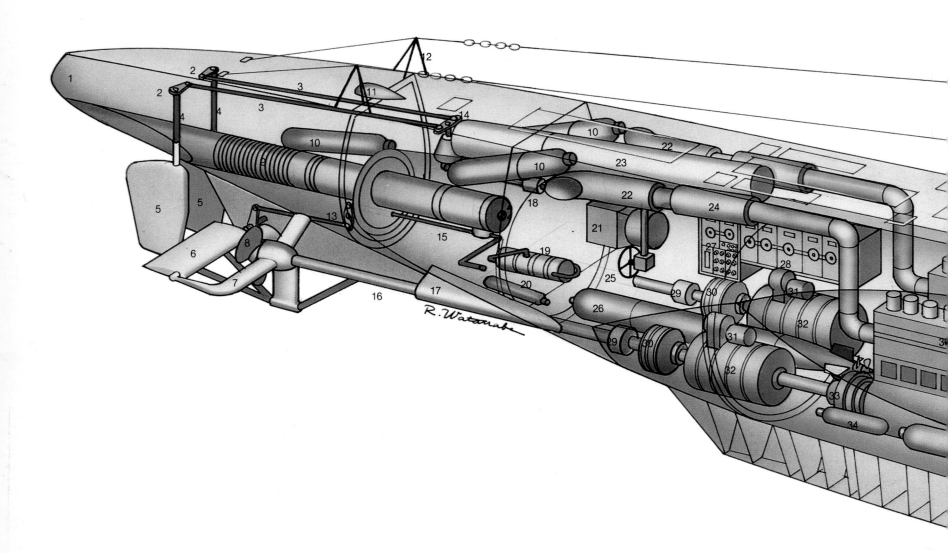

R. Watanabe

1. Stern casing
2. Rudder post universal joints
3. Rudder linkages
4. Rudder posts
5. Rudders
6. Aft starboard hydroplane
7. Rudder post
8. Starboard propeller
9. Stern torpedo tube
10. High pressure air bottles
11. Navigation light cover
12. Fixed deck rails
13. Hydroplane control linkage
14. Rudder control linkage
15. Hydroplane control arm
16. Propeller shaft
17. Propeller shaft housing/wartertight gland
18. Rudder control motor
19. Air compressor
20. Oxygen bottle
21. Auxiliary pump
22. Diesel exhaust outlets
23. Stern reserve torpedo container
24. Exhaust silencers
25. Rudder control wheel
26. Reserve torpedo
27. Port battery status panel
28. Port main electrical control panel
29. Oiling glands for propeller shafts
30. Main reduction gear boxes/clutches

31. Auxiliary generators
32. Main electric motors
33. Engine gear box/clutch
34. High pressure oxygen bottle
35. High pressure air supply to starboard engine starter
36. Germaniawerft 6-cylinder 4-stroke F46 diesel engines (with superchargers)
37. High pressure air bottle
38. Air inlet trunking
39. Air inlet control valve
40. Engine starters
41. Air inlet bleeder valve
42. Galley
43. Galley access/escape hatch
44. Keel
45. Access escape hatch
46. Senior nates' mess and quarters
47. High pressure air bottle
48. Aft battery room
49. Radio antennas
50. Insulators
51. Ensign staff
52. Gun platform guard rail
53. 20 mm C30 cannon
54. Elevation control wheels
55. Air inlets to diesel inlet system

56. Attack periscope
57. DF loop antenna
58. Control room/air search periscope
59. Attack periscope outer housing
60. Tower access/escape hatch
61. Bridge spray deflector
62. Wave deflector
63. Guard rails
64. Main magnetic compass
65. Propeller shaft revolution repeater
66. Attack computer
67. Access hatch to tower
68. Periscope control wheel
69. Boat surface air inlet mast
70. Diesel surface air inlet mast
71. Main diving tank pump
72. Aft bulkhead
73. Watertight hatch
74. Main control station for all diving and trim tanks
75. Auxiliary pump controls

U570 (Type VIIC) surrendered after having been damaged by a Hudson of No. 269 Squadron, RAF Coastal Command in the Atlantic on 27 August 1941. The photograph was taken from Catalina which relieved the Hudson. (Imperial War Museum)

British 250 lb (113 kg) Mk XI aerial depth charge

1. High explosive filling
2. Primer
3. Striker assembly
4. Spring
5. Pistol
6. Tail fins
7. Ring strut

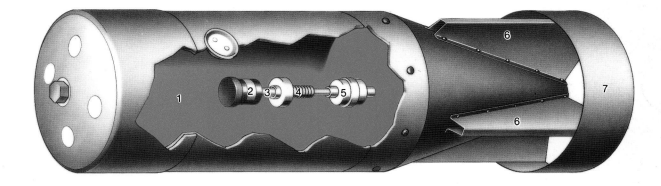

rines caused any serious damage. At this time it was estimated that only one attack in a hundred by British aircraft resulted in the submarine being assessed as "definitely sunk," while in a further two and a half attacks in each hundred, the boat was assessed as "probably sunk." There were two ways in which the effectiveness of a depth charge of a given size and weight could be improved. The first was to use a more powerful explosive, and this led to the use of the new Torpex explosive. Secondly, the explosive could be detonated closer to the hull of the submarine. In Britain work started on the development of a magnetic proximity fuse for depth charges, which would set them off during their descent through the water as they were at their closest point to the submarine.

While the development of the magnetic proximity fuse was in progress, Professor E. Williams of the Coastal Command operational research section conducted a painstaking examination of the records and photographs of attacks on U-boats. His efforts produced an interesting conclusion: that the reason the depth charges inflicted so little damage was that they usually detonated too far underneath their target. At that time the hydrostatic pistols were set to fire the charge at a depth between 100 and 150 ft (30 and 45 m), which was the *average*

depth a U-boat might reach by the time of the attack if it initiated its crash-dive at the *average* distance at which the aircraft was likely to be seen. But, as Williams pointed out, under these *average* conditions the boat was usually so far away from its diving swirl at the time of the attack that it was likely to escape anyway. The only submarines likely to be depth charged accurately were those surprised on the surface or in the act of submerging, and the depth charges were going off too far underneath these "easy" targets to inflict fatal damage. The photographs revealed that several boats had been caught on the surface and straddled with depth charges but they survived, albeit with a severe shaking.

William's analysis was a classic example of the value of operational analysis in time of war. It showed that what was needed was not a completely new weapon in the form of a proximity fused anti-submarine bomb—which would have been difficult and expensive to develop and could not reach service for more than a year—but a more realistic setting for the hydrostatic pistols of the depth charges already in use.

The last of the main areas that required improvement, if the British maritime patrol aircraft were to operate to maximum effect, was that of Intelligence on the whereabouts of

U-boats. Once this was known the aircraft could concentrate their patrols in those areas where enemy submarines were likely to be found. Since the beginning of the war, the Government Code and Cypher School at Bletchley Park near London had been conducting a long-running assault on the German and Italian radio cipher systems, and by the summer of 1940, this inspired work began to bear fruit. By May 1941 the chain of British radio intercept stations was receiving every signal transmitted from or to U-boats, and many of those signals were being deciphered and passed to the U-boat Tracking Room at the Admiralty in London. Included in these signals were the positions U-boats were to make for when forming patrol lines and a host of other information that made them vulnerable to attack.

The information from decrypted signals provided Royal Navy Intelligence officers with an immensely valuable insight into German Navy operational methods, but during 1941 it rarely had a decisive influence on the day-to-day fighting of convoy battles. There were two reasons for this: the delays in decrypting many of the signals, and the shortage of forces that could effectively exploit the information.

Although those working at Bletchley Park strove continually to shorten the time needed to decipher enemy signals, their task was extremely difficult, and there were often delays of a week or more between the time a signal was received and when it was read. In that time the tactical situation might have passed the point where such information had any tactical value. For example, on 19 May 1941 the eastbound convoy HX126 ran into a U-boat pack and lost eight ships in rapid succession; the German Naval command had broadcast the signal ordering the U-boats to their patrol line in front of the convoy on 14 May, and this was received by a British monitoring station, but the signal was not deciphered and read until 21 May. By then, it was too late to have any effect on the action.

Even when signals were decrypted in time, the lack of long-range patrol aircraft able to reach the mid-Atlantic prevented attacks on U-boat concentrations in that area. Often the most that could be done was to pass orders to re-route convoys safely clear of the German patrol lines. As yet the maritime patrol aircraft was unable to exploit the bonanza of Intelligence information on the U-boats which was now available. But, as we have observed, work was well in hand to remedy those deficiencies.

By the middle of 1941 Coastal Command's squadrons operated some 400 aircraft of all types. That was only one-third more than at the beginning of the war, but the quality of the aircraft was considerably better. Gone were the obsolete Ansons and biplane flying boats, their places taken by the far more effective Hudson, Wellington, and Whitley bombers. Many more Sunderlands were available, as were 30 American Catalina flying boats able to spend two hours on patrol at a distance of 800 miles (1,480 km) from base. About three-quarters of these aircraft were fitted with ASV radar, and the older types of anti-submarine bombs had been replaced by the more effective depth charges. Trials were progressing with the Leigh Light, but it was not yet ready for production. One squadron was about to form with American-built Liberator bombers which would be able to patrol for a similar time at more than 1,000 miles (1,850 km) from base.

By now the air patrols in the areas around the British Isles and the sea areas to the west were strong enough to force the German Wolf Packs to conduct their operations against convoys far out in the Atlantic. Until its Liberator squadron was ready for action, Coastal Command concentrated its shorter-range aircraft on patrols of the U-boat transit routes: through the Bay of Biscay for submarines moving to and from their bases in France, between Scotland and Iceland against boats moving out from Germany or Norway.

One of twenty Consolidated Liberator Mk Is (LB-30Bs) just after take off. (Imperial War Museum)

A Consolidated PBY-5 Catalina of U.S. Navy Patrol Squadron flying over the ocean in May 1942. Note radar antennas on the fuselage and wings. (National Archives)

An alternative to long-range aircraft to cover shipping passing through the "Atlantic Gap" was to use short-range aircraft operating from aircraft carriers. The Royal Navy possessed too few large carriers to hazard them in anti-submarine operations in the Atlantic, but in September 1941 the first of the so-called "Escort Carriers," HMS *Audacity*, began operations. A 5,500-ton freighter fitted with a small flight deck, arrester gear, and a simple crash barrier, *Audacity* carried six Martlet fighters which when not flying had to be parked on deck. *Audacity* was used to escort convoys passing between the United Kingdom and Gibraltar. Her aircraft's primary role was to drive away German long-range bombers and patrol aircraft. During her fourth such voyage, however, in December 1941, the convoy ran into a Wolf Pack, and the carrier's Martlets proved invaluable in forcing U-boats to dive and lose contact. During one of several night attacks, *Audacity* was torpedoed and sunk, but before she went down she demonstrated the value of the small, cheap carrier for anti-submarine operations.

Because maritime patrol aircraft lacked any effective means of illuminating U-boats on the surface, if the air patrols became too intense, the German sailors could cross dangerous stretches of water on the surface by night and continue their voyage moving rather slower but in perfect safety submerged during the day. As a result the air patrols over the transit routes

were able to account for only one boat during the year, *U206*, sunk by a Whitley of No. 502 Squadron on 30 November.

Although accurate night attacks on submarines were beyond the capability of most British aircraft at the end of 1941, during November and December a Fleet Air Arm unit demonstrated that they were possible for well trained crews if conditions were ideal. No. 812 Squadron was operating its Swordfish from North Front airfield, Gibraltar, against U-boats attempting to move from the Atlantic into the Mediterranean on the surface at night. The squadron's crews had considerable experience in night operations using ASV radar, and they developed a technique of homing on a radar contact until it disappeared in the sea clutter, and then holding their heading with both crewmen looking outside their open cockpits until they sighted the wake from the U-boat. In the clear skies over the Strait, this technique worked, and in a period of just over three weeks, the squadron's crews sank *U451* and inflicted serious damage on five other boats.

In December 1941, the Japanese attack on Pearl Harbor brought the USA into the war. At that time the U.S. Navy maritime patrol squadrons flew ASV II-fitted Hudsons and Catalinas, aircraft similar to those operated by the Royal Air Force. The Army Air Force operated B-18 bombers in this role. The U.S. forces received full information on British equipment

A U.S. Navy blimp armed with depth charges on convoy patrol over the North Atlantic on 3 January 1944. (National Archives)

and operating techniques, but they would take time to assimilate the new-found knowledge.

One type of maritime patrol vehicle unique to the U.S. Navy was the non-rigid airship, the blimp. At the outbreak of war about 20 of these unusual machines were operational. The most numerous type in service was the K Class, 251 ft (76.5 m) long and powered by two 425 hp engines which gave it a top speed of 55 mph (88.5 km/h). The blimp carried a crew of ten, ASV radar, and a war load of four 375 lb (170 kg) depth charges. At the time there was considerable debate about the blimp's operational value, and throughout the conflict they failed to destroy a single enemy submarine. However the blimps did have a considerable deterrent value, and in the thousands of convoys they escorted, no ship was ever lost to direct attack from an enemy submarine.

In January 1942 the first wave of five U-boats arrived off the east coast of the USA to find the American ships vulnerable beyond the wildest German dreams. At any one time there

were more than 100 ships plying through those waters; yet there were no convoys, no organized shipping routes, and few escorting ships and aircraft to hinder the attackers. It would take some months for the U.S. Navy and Army Air Forces to organize effective air patrols in the area and to introduce a system of convoys for merchant ships, and during that time many hundreds of thousands of tons of shipping were lost. For the U-boat crews, this was the second "Happy Time."

Thus far in the conflict the U-boats' main operating area in the mid-Atlantic had been beyond the reach of Allied maritime patrol aircraft, and these aircraft could not attack U-boats on the surface as a matter of course. Because of these limitations it was a relatively simple matter for U-boat crews to avoid attack from the air, and the aircraft exerted only minimal pressure on German submarine operations. When they encountered submarines within their range, the aircraft had shown that they could sometimes find, intimidate, and wound submarines, but only on rare occasions were they able to sink them.

The Fight Avails

During the first half of 1942, the strength of the naval and air patrols around the east coast of the USA increased to the point where there were no longer easy pickings for the German and Italian submariners in that area. Instead, they resumed their battle against the convoys passing through the "Atlantic Gap" where there was little or no interference to their operations from patrolling aircraft.

Even in the mid-Atlantic the easy times for the U-boat crews were starting to draw to an end, however. Since the autumn of 1941 No. 120 Squadron of the Royal Air Force had been operational, its very-long-range Liberators able to spend up to three hours on patrol 1,100 miles (2,040 km) from base, carrying eight 250 lb (113 kg) depth charges. Initially the Liberators were fully employed in extended-range reconnaissance operations searching for German blockade runners and other shipping, and in support of Allied convoys carrying supplies to Russia. It was August 1942 before the Squadron began flying regular patrols in support of convoys passing through the "Atlantic Gap." During these operations the Liberators of No. 120 Squadron had frequent encounters with U-boats, and some of these are described elsewhere in this book in the separate stories of aircraft AM929 and Squadron Leader Terry Bulloch. On several occasions the timely arrival of a single aircraft over a convoy was sufficient to disrupt a Wolf Pack of 20 or more U-boats preparing to launch an attack.

More New Equipment

With the entry of the USA into the war, that nation's massive industrial capacity was switched to a war footing. The brief career of HMS *Audacity* had shown that one of the most effective ways of protecting convoys from attack by enemy submarines and aircraft was to provide them with air cover from escort carriers. Accordingly the U.S. Navy initiated a program to build large numbers of these small, relatively cheap aircraft carriers. During the Allied landings in Morocco and Algeria in November 1942, six such carriers formed part of the escort for the invasion force, and after the initial landings, these provided support for the troops ashore. Throughout these operations the aircraft from the escort carriers did not encounter any U-boats, however. They were a hazard the German and Italian submariners would have to face, but later.

Scientists and technicians in the USA, Britain, and Canada took part in a series of coordinated programs to develop new detection and location devices and weapons to assist aircraft to defeat the U-boat. Five such systems, all of which involved major advances in technology, were given priority status and were well into their flight trials by the close of 1942: the centimetric wavelength ASV radar, the sonobuoy, the "Mark 24 Mine" homing torpedo, the magnetic airborne detector, and its associated retrobomb.

The newly developed centimetric wavelength radar gave considerably better range and definition than the earlier sets (ASV Mark II operated on a wavelength of 1.7 m). Moreover, the centimetric wavelength transmissions could be focused into a very fine beam and radiated from a rotating scanner to cover the surface in a full 360-degree circle around the aircraft. The new type of radar promised a huge increase in

The centimetric wavelength radar H2S fitted to de Havilland Mosquito B Mk16 for night bombing. (Imperial War Museum)

capability for night fighters and bombers as well as maritime patrol aircraft; however, as the former had a higher priority, several months would pass before the first of the new radars were allocated to anti-submarine units. The first centimetric wavelength ASV radars fitted to maritime patrol aircraft began operational trials towards the end of 1942.

Radar could locate a submarine only if it exposed part of its structure above the surface. To detect and locate a submerged boat from the air, quite different systems were required. One such device was the sonobuoy, a small floating radio transmitter under which a hydrophone was suspended on a length of cable. Developed by the U.S. Navy, the first sonobuoy was designated the AN/CRT-1 and went into production in the USA towards the end of 1942. The device comprised a cylindrical buoy 3 ft 9 in (1.14 m) long, 4 in (10.2 cm) in diameter, and weighing 14 lb (6.35 kg). After release from the aircraft, a parachute opened to slow its fall, and on impact with the water, the hydrophone was released from the base of the cylinder and sank to the limit of the 24-foot (7.3 m) connecting cable. Under ideal conditions, with calm seas and the submarine moving at high speed, the hydrophone could pick up the propeller noises at distances up to 3½ miles (6.5 km), but under operational conditions in the North Atlantic, the range of the device would usually be considerably less. After amplification the sounds picked up by the hydrophone were passed by radio to the aircraft, where one of the crew had the usually difficult task of sorting the sounds of the submarine from the many and varied noises produced by the sea and the creatures in it. AN/CRT-1 gave no indication of the direction of the source of the noises received, so to get even an approximate indication of the location of the submarine, it was necessary for the aircraft to lay a pattern of five sonobuoys around its suspected position.

Even under ideal conditions a sonobuoy pattern would give only a rough indication of the position of a submerged U-boat. To enable the aircraft to attack the boat thus found, some form of homing weapon was needed, and during 1942 U.S. Navy scientists developed one. The device, designated the "Mark 24 Mine" to conceal its true purpose, was a torpedo which homed on the propeller noises from the submarine. Under ideal conditions it could do so from a maximum range of about ¾ mile (1.4 km). At the end of 1942 the Mark 24 Mine was placed in production, the first self-homing guided missile in the world to achieve this status.

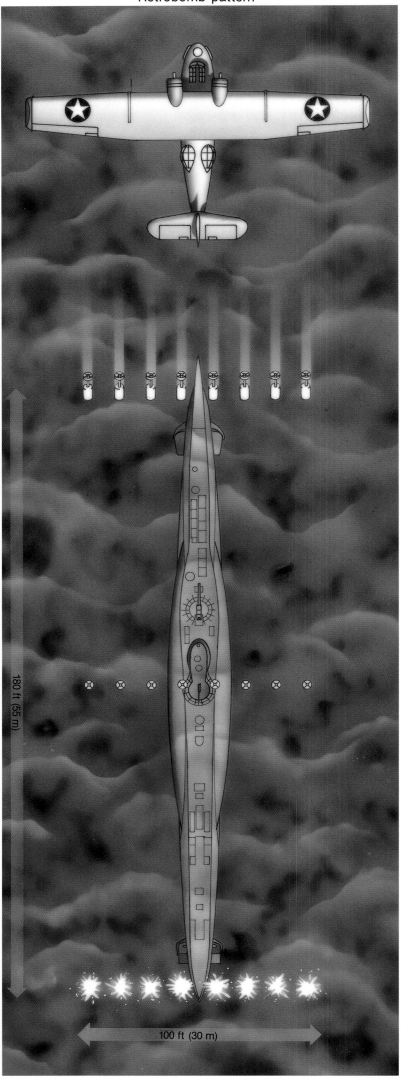

Retrobomb pattern

180 ft (55 m)

100 ft (30 m)

Such were the difficulties of attacking submerged U-boats from the air that no single system was judged to provide the complete answer to the problem. A second quite separate system was also developed in the USA for this purpose, the Magnetic Airborne Detector (MAD) and its associated retrobomb weapon. Built by the Western Electric Company and the Airborne Instruments Laboratory under a U.S. Navy contract, MAD employed a sensitive magnetometer to measure the distortion of the earth's magnetic field caused by a nearby ferrous metallic object—such as a submarine. Flight trials showed that MAD could detect a submarine beneath the surface to a maximum distance of 400 ft (120 m), but that meant to detect a boat 300 ft (90 m) beneath the sea, the aircraft had to be 100 ft (30 m) above the surface. Moreover the device indicated the presence of the U-boat only when the aircraft was immediately over it, which gave rise to a fundamental problem: if the stick of normal depth charges was released on the MAD indication from an aircraft flying at 100 knots (185 km/h), the forward throw of the weapons would carry them safely clear of the target. To overcome this difficulty the California Institute of Technology developed a specialized weapon for use with MAD: the retrobomb weighing 35 lb (16 kg), which carried a small rocket motor fitted in the tail. During an operational attack the MAD could be set to fire the retrobombs *automatically* when a U-boat was detected. On receipt of a firing signal, the rocket in each bomb propelled it *rearwards* off its launching rail under the wing of the aircraft, which cancelled the forward speed of the weapon and allowed it to fall *vertically* into the sea. If during its passage through the water a bomb struck the submarine, an impact fuse detonated its shaped-charge warhead. To give a reasonable chance of scoring one or more such hits, the aircraft released its entire load of 24 retrobombs during a single attack, thus laying a pattern of bombs over the target.

By the end of 1942 all of these new devices were either operational or on the point of becoming operational. But more months would pass before they would start to have any influence on the course of the war against the U-boat.

The Cipher-Breakers Succeed

In contrast to the new types of weapon under development, successes by the cipher-breakers were likely to have immediate and far-reaching consequences. During 1942 the techniques for breaking into the German machine ciphers had been refined greatly, but while there had been considerable success against those of the German Army and the *Luftwaffe*, those used by the German Navy had stubbornly resisted most of their efforts. Indeed, during that year the German Navy had introduced a modification to its cipher machines which safeguarded the contents of many of its signals for several months. Then, in December 1942, the main cipher used to control U-boat operations was finally broken. From then on progressively more and more of the German signals were read, sometimes in time for the information to have a bearing on the control of anti-U-boat operations. The mastery of the German Navy ciphers gradually became total, and from August 1943 until the end of the war, all U-boat traffic was read as a matter of course with little or no delay.

The importance of the information obtained from decrypted signals can scarcely be exaggerated. Unless it was sailing on a special task or to a distant area, a U-boat would receive its

A 20 mm MG C30 anti-aircraft cannon mounted on the platform of *U74* (Type VIIB). (Bundesarchiv)

destination point and operational orders by signal when it was at sea. Often the destination point was its position in a patrol line, and the collation of several such signals provided the eavesdroppers with the limits of the line and the exact extent of the area around which an approaching convoy had to be re-routed to avoid it. No U-boat could deviate from its orders without first requesting and receiving permission to do so, and when it signaled headquarters, each boat had to give its position. Any boat which did not transmit for several days received an order from headquarters to report its position, and this was repeated several times until it did so; the failure of a boat to answer such a demand was usually a clear indication that it had been sunk. As a result of this bonanza of absolutely reliable and up-to-the-minute information on the workings of the enemy force, the Allied U-boat Tracking Rooms could now dispose their forces to ensure they had maximum effect against the German Wolf Packs.

Improvements to the U-boats

While these developments to counter the U-boat had been in train, the German Navy saw clearly the need to produce new types of submarines which would be less vulnerable to

detection and attack from the air. One of the first moves, initiated late in 1942, was to fit all new boats with a platform aft of the conning tower for a 20 mm anti-aircraft gun; older boats undergoing refit were modified to take the new mounting.

Also at this time the German Navy pressed ahead with the development of the Schnorkel, an air pipe which could be raised above the surface when the U-boat was running at periscope depth. Drawing air through the Schnorkel, a boat could run at this depth on its diesel engines indefinitely without depleting the limited charge in its batteries. The Schnorkel had its shortcomings: if the sea was rough or the depth-keeping poor, water washing over the air inlet would cause the ball cock to slam shut. If that happened the crew of the boat was in for an uncomfortable time: unless they were immediately shut down, the diesel engines continued to suck in their quota of air, causing a sudden fall of pressure in the boat which left the crewmen gasping in an agony of popping ears and bulging eyes. But this limitation was more than balanced by the fact that it was far more difficult for aircraft to detect a Schnorkeling U-boat than one on the surface recharging its batteries in the normal way. The small air pipe extending above the surface could sometimes be seen visually or on radar, but such detection was possible only at short range and then only if the sea was relatively calm. Late in 1943 the Schnorkel was ordered into production; plans were laid to fit the device to all new U-boats and install it in older boats on refit.

The decision to fit anti-aircraft guns and Schnorkels to the boats currently in service was seen as a short-term measure to enable them to continue operating perhaps until the end of 1944. By then the German Navy hoped to introduce three new types of U-boat with much better underwater speeds and ranges than their predecessors, boats which would be less vulnerable to attack from the air: the Type XVII, the Type XXI, and the Type XXIII.

Head of a schnorkel

1. Air intake
2. Safety valve
3. Float
4. Exhaust gas mast
5. Exhaust gas exit
6. Exhaust gas
7. Air intake mast
8. Air

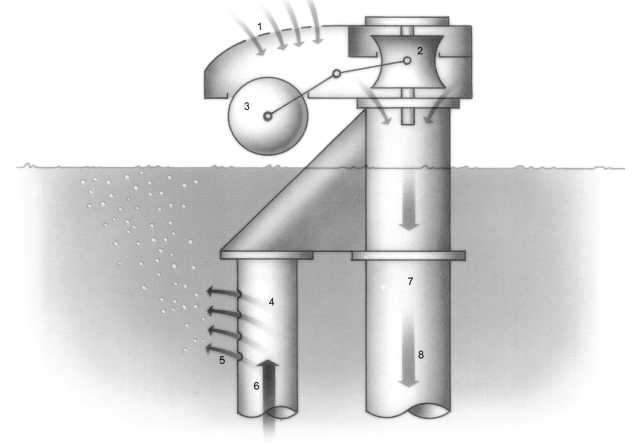

Type XXI U-boat

Displacement	Max speed	Armament
Surfaced: 1,621 tons	Surfaced: 15.6 knots (28.9 km/h)	Bow torpedo tubes: 6
Submerged: 1,819 tons	Submerged: 17.2 knots (31.9 km/h)	Torpedoes carried: 23
Dimensions	**Range**	2 × twin 20 mm cannon
Length: 76.7 m (251 ft 7¾ in)	Surfaced: 11,150 nautical miles (20,650 km) at 12 knots (22.2 km/h)	**Air warning equipment**
Beam: 6.6 m (21 ft 7⅞ in)	Submerged: 285 nautical niles (528 km) at 6 knots (11.1 km/h)	FuMO 65 *Hohentwiel-Drauf* radar
Draught: 6.3 m (20 ft 8 in)	**Max operation depth**	Crew 57
Propulsion	150–200 m (490–660 ft), approx.	
Diesel engines: 2 × 2,000 hp		
Electric motors: 2 × 113 hp		

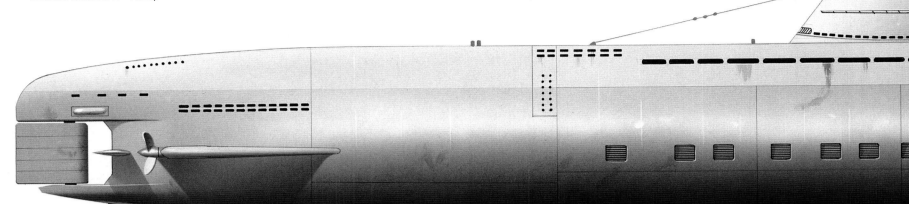

The Type XVII was a coastal patrol boat fitted with a novel method of propulsion fueled by hydrogen peroxide to give high speed and long endurance underwater; if the system proved successful, it would later be built into a newer and larger boat with ocean-going performance.

The Type XXI was a 1,500-ton ocean-goer with a battery capacity three times larger than that of any previous boat of similar size. As a result the new boat would have an excellent underwater performance: a maximum speed of 18 knots or a cruising speed of 6 knots for 48 hours, and an underwater range of nearly 300 miles (560 km) completely submerged, which could be extended by periodically recharging the batteries using the Schnorkel.

The Type XXIII was a small coastal boat with an enlarged battery capacity to give a high underwater performance, but it weighed only 232 tons, and its maximum range was only 1,300 miles (2,400 km).

Because of the urgency to get them into service, the three new types of U-boat were ordered "off the drawing board." To speed production, all three were to be built in pre-fabricated sections in factories throughout Germany, then brought together for rapid assembly at shipyards before launching. Their type designations were in reverse order of technical difficulty in getting each through its development phase and into large-scale production: the Type XVII had the greatest number of untried features; the Type XXI employed mainly proven techniques, but its size would give difficulties to those making and transporting the pre-fabricated sections; the Type XXIII was the smallest and simplest of the three to develop and produce, though this would take much longer than was optimistically predicted at the beginning of 1943.

The Decisive Convoy Battles: March and May 1943

While both sides were striving behind the scenes to introduce new equipment to improve their effectiveness in the conflict now evolving, for a little longer the battle between the convoys and the U-boats continued along the lines previously seen. Between 16 and 19 March 1943 the eastbound convoys, HX229 and SL122, were attacked by three packs of U-boats in the "Atlantic Gap." As a result 21 ships totaling 141,000 tons were sunk, with the loss of one U-boat. As a British Admiralty report later admitted: "The Germans never came so near disrupting communications between the New World and the Old as in the first 20 days of March 1943."

For the rest of March and most of April 1943, severe weather in the North Atlantic prevented military operations in that area, and the ships suffered a battering only from the sea. Then in May the weather improved, and both sides prepared for a resumption of the battle around the convoys. By then the Royal Air Force had two squadrons with some 30 very-long-range Liberators able to patrol in the "Atlantic Gap," and escort carriers would be available to support some of the convoys passing through that area. The additional protection would be needed if a massacre was to be prevented. Admiral Dönitz now had more than a hundred U-boats in the Atlantic, poised on their patrol lines ready to administer a repeat of the punishment meted out to HX229 and SC122 in March.

The first groups of Allied ships to enter the "Atlantic Gap" after the weather improved were the eastbound convoys HX237 and SC129, supported by a powerful naval escort which included the small aircraft carrier HMS *Biter* with nine Swordfish and three Wildcats. The action opened on the afternoon of 10 May when one of *Biter*'s Swordfish forced *U403* to lose contact with HX237 which it had been shadowing. Acting on information from de-crypted German signals, the convoys were routed round some of the U-boat concentrations, and there was no action on the 11th. But there were limits to what could be achieved by re-routing in submarine-infested waters, and on the morning of the 12th the action resumed as the U-boats closed on their prey. The convoys now received additional support in the shape of three very-long-range Liberators of No. 86 Squadron, each carrying one of the new "Mark 24 Mine" homing torpedoes in addition to the normal depth charges. Flight Lieu-

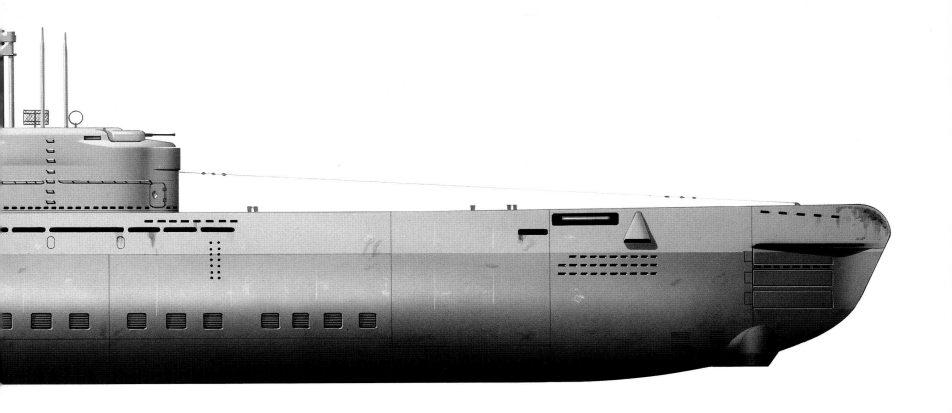

tenant J. Wright dropped his torpedo into the diving swirl left by *U456* as she submerged on the approach of the aircraft. Two minutes and several hundred yards later, there was a small upheaval in the water as the 100 lb (45 kg) warhead detonated against the U-boat and caused serious damage. Warships escorting the convoy finished off the crippled boat the next day. Fortified with continuous cover throughout the daylight hours from Liberators and aircraft from the escort carrier, the convoys fought their way past 36 enemy submarines and lost only five ships in exchange for four U-boats sunk and others damaged.

On 14 May, following the action around HX237 and SC129, aircraft made two more attacks with homing torpedoes in the North Atlantic. A Liberator of No. 86 Squadron and a Catalina of U.S. Navy VP-84 (Patrol Squadron 84) released these weapons in separate attacks on U-boats which had dived, and in each case there was a mushroom-like disturbance in the water more than a minute later as the weapons detonated. No other result was seen, but from German records it is known that *U226* and *U657* disappeared without trace in positions which corresponded to these attacks.

Two Fairey Swordfish Mk II and a Hawker Sea Hurricane Mk IIC aboard the escort carrier HMS *Striker* during an anti-submarine sweep in 1944. Note 3 in armor-piercing rockets under the wings of Swordfish. (Imperial War Museum)

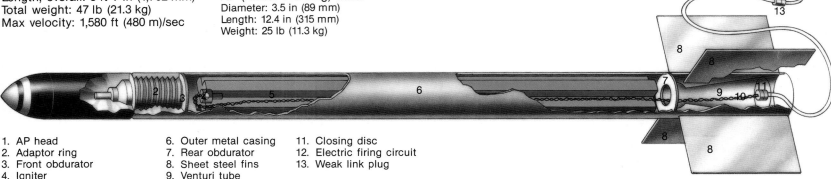

British 3 in rocket projectile

Length, overall: 5 ft 7 in (1,702 mm)
Total weight: 47 lb (21.3 kg)
Max velocity: 1,580 ft (480 m)/sec

AP (Armor Piercing) head
Diameter: 3.5 in (89 mm)
Length: 12.4 in (315 mm)
Weight: 25 lb (11.3 kg)

1. AP head
2. Adaptor ring
3. Front obdurator
4. Igniter
5. Crusiform shaped cordite
6. Outer metal casing
7. Rear obdurator
8. Sheet steel fins
9. Venturi tube
10. Igniter lead
11. Closing disc
12. Electric firing circuit
13. Weak link plug

At this time the lumbering Swordfish biplanes operating from escort carriers also received an effective new weapon for use against U-boats on the surface: the armor-piercing rocket. The Swordfish carried launchers for eight of these missiles under its wings and fired them in anger for the first time on 23 May. On that day Sub Lieutenant Harry Horrocks of No. 819 Squadron took off from HMS *Archer* to investigate a U-boat shadowing convoy HX239, and by adroit use of cloud cover managed to surprise *U752* on the surface. He fired his first pair of rockets from 800 yards (730 m) and saw them hit the water 150 yards (140 m) short of the target; his second pair, fired from 400 yards (370 m), fell 30 yards (27 m) short; the third pair, from 300 yards (270 m), struck the water ten yards (9 m) short; and the fourth pair, fired from 200 yards (180 m), scored hits on

the stern of the boat. These rockets were designed to be aimed into the water short of the target, however, and had heads shaped to give an upwards curving underwater trajectory to enable them to strike the U-boat beneath the water line. At least one of the rockets from Horrocks' third pair did just that: it struck *U752* on her No. 4 diving tank and punched clean through the pressure hull. A wide jet of water cascaded into the submarine, which wallowed on the surface, unable to dive, discharging large quantities of oil. Following a strafing attack by one of *Archer*'s Wildcat fighters, the German crew scuttled the crippled boat and was rescued by one of the convoy escorts.

The action around HX237 and SC129 proved to be the turning point in the Battle of the Atlantic; from now on the provision of almost continuous air patrols would render the "Atlan-

Grumman TBF-1C Avenger

of VC-55 aboard the USS *Card* (CVE-13) in the Atlantic, spring of 1943.

Power unit
Wright R-2600-8 14-cylinder air-cooled engine:
    1,700 hp for take-off
    1,450 hp at 12,000 ft (3,660 m)
Dimensions
Span: 54 ft 2 in (16.51 m)
Span, wings folded: 19 ft 0 in (5.79 m)
Length, tail up: 40 ft 11½ in (12.48 m)
Height, tail up: 16 ft 5 in (5.00 m)
Wing area: 490 sq ft (45.5 m²)
Weights
Empty: 10,555 lb (4,788 kg)
Gross: 16,412 lb (7,444 kg)

Ground crews loading 3 in AP rockets into the guide rails beneath the starboard wing of Bristol Beaufighter belonging to Coastal Command. (Imperial War Museum)

Performance
Max speed: 257 mph (414 km/h) at 12,000 ft (3,660 m)
Cruising speed: 153 mph (246 km/h)
Time to climb to 10,000 ft (3,050 m): 13 min
Service ceiling: 21,400 ft (6,520 m)
Range with 2,216 lb (1,005 kg) torpedo: 1,105 mls (1,780 km)
Armament
Fixed forward-firing: 2 × 0.50 in (12.7 mm) Browning M2 machine guns
Flexible mounted aft-firing:
  1 × 0.50 in (12.7 mm) Browning M2 machine gun and 1 × 0.30 in (7.62 mm)
  Browning M2 machine gun
Bombs/depth charges: up to 2,000 lb (910 kg)
Forward-firing rockets: 8 × 3.5 in (89 mm)
Crew 3

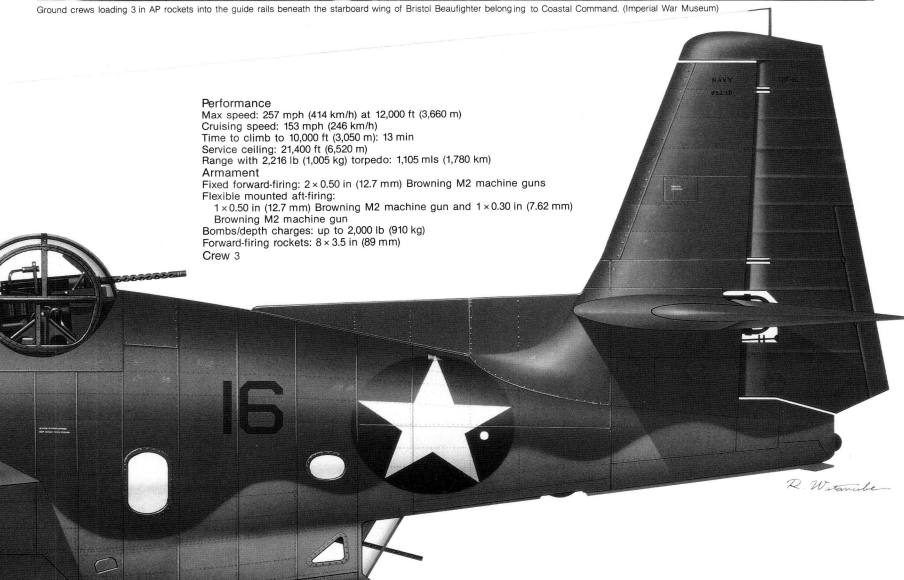

Fairey Swordfish Mk II Cutaway

1. Fixed tab
2. Elevator structure
3. Tail navigation light (white)
4. Elevator control horn
5. Rudder structure
6. Antenna mast
7. Bracing wire attachment
8. External bracing wire
9. Lashing down shackle
10. Fixed tailwheel
11. Elevator and rudder control cables
12. Longerons
13. Upper aileron structure
14. Arresting hook pivot
15. Arresting hook (extended)
16. Upper wing rear spar
17. Starboard navigation light (green)
18. Upper wing front spar
19. Rear catapult spool
20. Ballast weights
21. Radio installation
22. Reserve drum magazines
23. Gunner's seat
24. Machine gun stowage trough
25. 0.303 in (7.7 mm) Lewis machine gun
26. Fairey high-speed flexible gun mounting
27. Antenna
28. Inter-cockpit fairing
29. Antenna mast
30. Pilot's head rest
31. Pilot's seat
32. 0.303 in (7.7 mm) Vickers machine gun (starboard only)
33. Windscreen
34. Flap control handwheel
35. Dinghy release cord
36. Dinghy release cord handle
37. Identification light
38. Type C dinghy stowage
39. Fixed tab
40. Upper aileron
41. Aileron hinge
42. Port navigation light (red)
43. Leading-edge slots
44. Pitot tube
45. ASV Mk II antennas
46. Interplane struts
47. Flying wires
48. Bracing wires
49. External torpedo sight bars
50. Fuel filler caps
51. Fuel gravity tank (12.5 Imp gal/10.4 U.S. gal/56.8 ltr)
52. Main fuel tank (155 Imp gal/186 U.S. gal/705 ltr)
53. Oil cooler
54. Oil tank (13.75 Imp gal/16.51 U.S. gal/62.5 ltr)
55. Oil filler cap
56. Fire wall bulkhead
57. Engine support bearers
58. Cowling support ring
59. Cowling
60. Bristol Pegasus IIIM3 nine-cylinder air-cooled radial engine
61. Spinner
62. Three-blade fixed-pitch Fairey-Reed metal propeller
63. Exhaust collector ring
64. Cowling clips
65. Jacking foot
66. Main wheel
67. Dunlop main wheel tires
68. Flame-damper exhaust tailpipe extension
69. Radius rod fairing
70. Undercarriage axle tube fairing

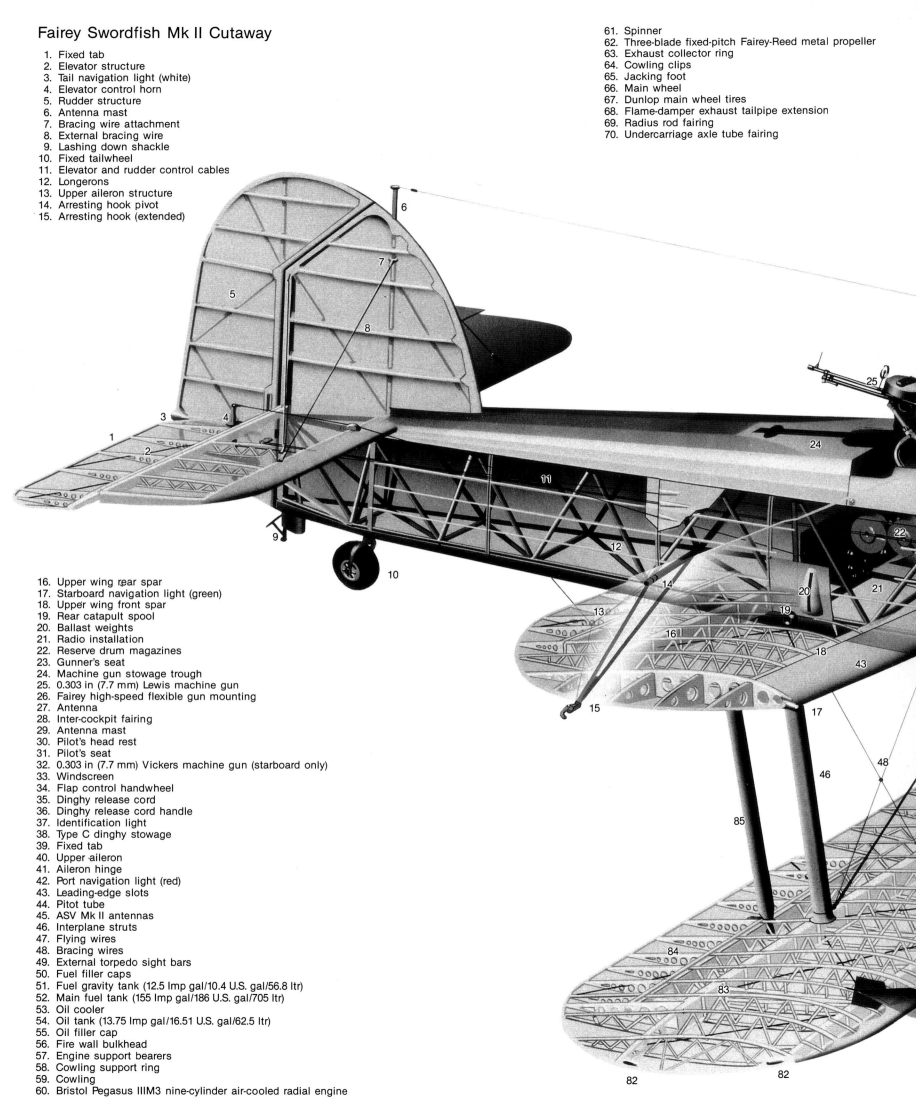

71. Wheel cover
72. Undercarriage oleo leg fairing
73. Wing locking handle
74. Air intake slot
75. Drag strut
76. Lower wing front spar
77. Rocket-launching rails
78. Underwing strengthening plate
79. 25 lb (11.3 kg) armor-piercing rocket projectiles
80. Underwing bomb shackles
81. 20 lb (9.1 kg) bombs
82. Deck-handling grips
83. Lower wing rear spar
84. Lower aileron structure
85. Aileron connect strut

tic Gap" a thing of the past. With exact and timely knowledge of the position and composition of each Wolf Pack forming or formed, those at the U-boat Tracking Rooms could direct escorting ships and aircraft into positions to stifle attempts to attack the convoys before they developed. During the period from 10 to 24 May, no fewer than ten convoys comprising some 370 merchant ships passed through the mid-Atlantic danger area losing only six ships. For this meager return the German submarine service lost 13 boats: seven to aircraft, two to aircraft working with naval escorts, and four to naval escorts operating alone. On 24 May Admiral Dönitz called a halt to the one-sided battle in the mid-Atlantic. He ordered some of the boats to form a new patrol line off the Azores, where the Allied defenses were thought to be less strong, and the rest to return to their bases in France.

The attack on convoys between the USA and North Africa as they sailed past the Azores brought only misery to the U-boat crews. Each of these convoys enjoyed the protection of an escort carrier, and the result was a "Happy Time" for the crews flying aircraft off the decks of the U.S. Navy carriers, *Bogue, Card, Core,* and *Santee. Santee* developed a technique of

mounting anti-submarine patrols using pairs of aircraft: an F4F Wildcat fighter to strafe the enemy boat and force it to submerge, and a TBF Avenger which would then plant a Mark 24 Mine homing torpedo in the diving swirl of any boat which did so. Using these tactics *Santee*'s aircraft sank three U-boats during July. During this phase of the battle, which extended through June, July, and August, aircraft from the four American carriers sank 13 U-boats; surface ships sank two more before the surviving U-boats withdrew, having failed to mount a single successful attack on any of the convoys.

More than anything else, the German commander knew he had to maintain his force until sufficient U-boats were fitted with Schnorkels, making them less vulnerable to air attack. Beyond that, he would need to preserve a hard core of trained crews to man the new types of U-boat when they started coming off the slipways. Then he could resume the fight with renewed vigor. Yet even as the surviving U-boats were on their way home after their defeat in the mid-Atlantic, a separate and quite different sort of battle with patrol aircraft was nearing its climax in the Bay of Biscay.

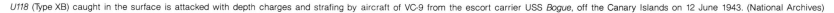
U118 (Type XB) caught in the surface is attacked with depth charges and strafing by aircraft of VC-9 from the escort carrier USS *Bogue*, off the Canary Islands on 12 June 1943. (National Archives)

The Battle of the Bay

While the battle between aircraft and submarines ran to its climax in the mid-Atlantic, another equally hard-fought action was running its course in the waters off the west coast of France: the Battle of the Bay. The Bay referred to was the Bay of Biscay, the strip of water contained between Brest on the northwest coast of France and Cape Ortegal on the northwest coast of Spain. The waterway is some 300 miles (560 km) wide, and through it passed three out of every four German and Italian submarines on their way to and from their operating areas in the Atlantic. Obviously the Bay was likely to be a fruitful hunting area for patrol aircraft, especially since it was within easy reach of Coastal Command's medium range aircraft which initially comprised by far the greater part of its force. As Coastal Command gradually built up its strength, the air patrols over the Bay became more and more threatening. But the U-boat crews soon learned that if the aircraft became too bothersome, it was easy enough to avoid them by the simple expedient of crossing the area submerged by day or on the surface at night.

The submarine's virtual immunity to night attack from the air was to come to an end in June 1942, however. At the beginning of that month, No. 172 Squadron of the Royal Air Force possessed five Wellingtons fitted with Leigh Lights, and its crews had completed training for the difficult and precise flying necessary to carry out attacks on targets illuminated by the searchlight.

The first attack using the Leigh Light took place on the morning of 4 June, when Squadron Leader Jeaff Greswell and his crew caught the Italian submarine *Luigi Torelli* on the surface in the Bay of Biscay. Greswell put down his depth charges close to the submarine held in the beam of light and damaged the boat sufficiently to force her to turn back for France.

In June 1942, crews from No. 172 Squadron made contact with six other enemy submarines and attacked five of them. The Leigh Light caused the destruction of its first U-boat during the early morning darkness on 6 July, when Pilot Officer W. Howell and his crew caught *U502* as she was returning from a successful foray in the Caribbean. Eight days later this crew carried out another successful Leigh Light attack which inflicted serious damage on *U159*.

Initially there were only five searchlight-fitted Wellingtons available for operations, but they had an effect far beyond the one submarine sunk and two damaged during June and July 1942. The immunity enjoyed by U-boat crews traversing the Bay of Biscay on the surface at night had gone; instead, they were now liable to devastating attacks suddenly and without warning. The German sailors coined their own name for the Leigh Light: *das verdammte Licht*—"that damned light."

Admiral Dönitz over-reacted to the new situation, and on 16 July he issued orders to his boats that they were to reverse their previous procedure from crossing the Bay. From now on they were to cross the stretch of water submerged at night and *on the surface by day*. The change of tactics gave the daylight air patrols their chance, and they seized it, with the result that there were 34 sightings of U-boats in the Bay area in August and 37 in September. Between the beginning of June and the end of September, only four boats were sunk in the area, but during the five months previously there had been none.

After analyzing the British tactics, German Naval officers realized that the best way to counter them was to fit all U-boats with a simple radio receiver that would pick up the signals from ASV II radar. Thus warned of the presence of an enemy patrol aircraft in their area, the boats could dive to safety before an attack could develop. The warning receiver, known as the *Metox*, was introduced in September 1942, and by the end of the year, nearly every U-boat carried one. The warnings from *Metox* effectively restored the cloak of invisibility to the U-boats at night. During September there were only two sightings of boats in the Bay at night, and in October there were none at all.

The introduction of the *Metox* receiver effectively prevented night attacks on U-boats by Leigh Light Wellingtons fitted with ASV II. But by the end of 1942, two new and much

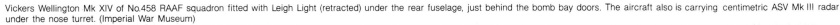

Vickers Wellington Mk XIV of No.458 RAAF squadron fitted with Leigh Light (retracted) under the rear fuselage, just behind the bomb bay doors. The aircraft also is carrying centimetric ASV Mk III radar under the nose turret. (Imperial War Museum)

Type VIIC/41 U-boat with a schnorkel in 1944

Armament
1 × 37 mm cannon
2 × twin 20 mm cannon
Air warning equipment
FuMO 61 *Hohentwiel* U radar
FuMB 7 *Naxos* detecting receiver

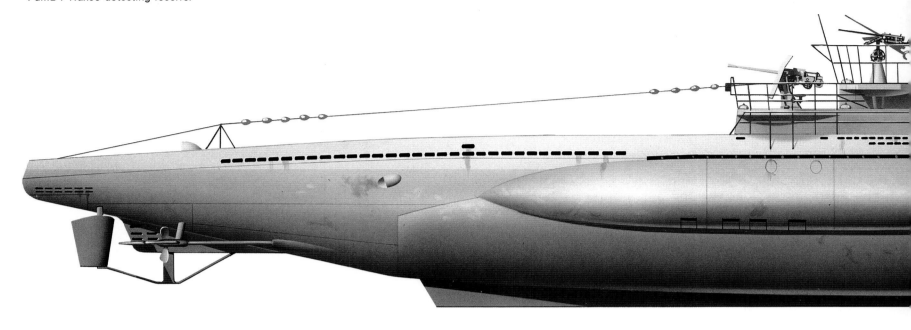

more advanced types of ASV radar were ready to go into service: the British ASV Mark III and the American SCR 517. Not only could the new types of radar detect submarines on the surface and convoys at significantly greater distances than the older radar, but significantly for this account, their operating frequencies in the 3,000 Megahertz band were far outside the range of cover of the *Metox*, so the German sailors would receive no warning from the receiver if an aircraft fitted with the new radar was running in to attack them.

No. 172 Squadron began night operations against the U-boats using the ASV Mark III radar in March 1943. Immediately there was a return of the night attacks without warning, which had been so devastating to morale. During March and April only two U-boats were sunk at night in the Bay, but the crews of several others returned with hair-raising tales of narrow escapes. Pending the introduction of a warning receiver which could pick up the signals from the new Allied radars, at the end of April Admiral Dönitz ordered that boats passing through the Bay of Biscay should do so submerged at night or if visibility was poor, and run on the surface only if the skies were clear. In a further change of tactics, he ordered that boats caught on the surface and unable to dive in time to avoid attack from the air were to fight back against their tormentors. To provide the means to do so, during their time in port between sorties, boats were fitted with twin- and even quadruple-barreled 20 mm cannon in place of the previous single-barreled weapons.

The change in German tactics immediately became obvious to those conducting air patrols over the Bay of Biscay by day; during the first week in May, U-boats were sighted on 71 occasions and attacked on 43, resulting in the destruction of three boats and damage to three others. Moreover, returning aircrews reported 17 occasions when U-boats remained on the surface and tried to defend themselves with anti-aircraft fire.

Initially the U-boats' "fight back" tactics were not effective; the fire-power of a single boat was insufficient to deter a determined aircrew from attacking. In May aircraft sank six U-boats in the Bay of Biscay area and severely damaged six more, with the loss of six aircraft shot down. That put the balance overwhelmingly in favor of Coastal Command. On average an aircraft cost about a fifth the price of a U-boat, and it carried about one-eighth as many crewmen.

By the beginning of June almost all U-boats leaving the French ports for the Atlantic carried batteries of anti-aircraft guns, and Admiral Dönitz ordered a further change in tactics. U-boats were now to cross the Bay of Biscay in broad daylight in groups; if enemy aircraft approached, the sailors had strict orders that they were not to submerge. Instead they were to use their combined firepower to drive away or shoot down the Allied aircraft. When darkness fell, the U-boats were to submerge and continue their transit at a prescribed speed; at dawn they were to surface, re-form their group, and continue as before until they were clear of the Bay.

At first it seemed that the new group sailing tactics might have solved the problem of getting the U-boats through the Bay without excessive losses. A pair of boats returning from patrol reached Brest safety on 7 June, as did a second pair on the 11th. Late on the afternoon of the 12th, an aircraft sighted the first of the large U-boat groups to attempt to run the gauntlet: five boats moving on the surface on their way to the Atlantic. Darkness fell before an attack could be launched, and as ordered, the U-boats continued their westward passage submerged. On the following evening a patroling Sunderland of No. 228 Squadron sighted the group and, undeterred by the hail of return fire, carried out an accurate attack on *U564* before it was hit and crashed into the sea. With severe damage *U564* broke off her patrol and, escorted by *U185*, returned to her

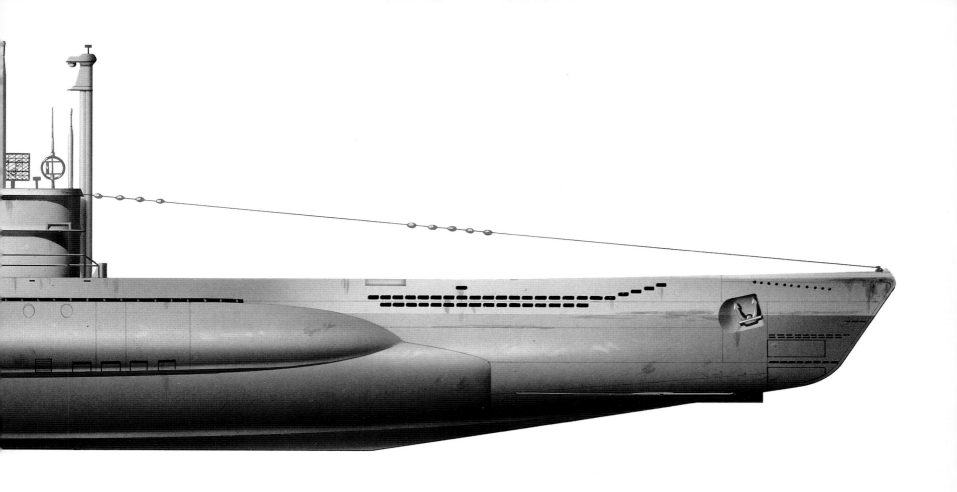

U966 (Type VIIC) under air attack by a Liberator of RAF Coastal Command in the Atlantic, 1943. Increased anti-aircraft armament (four 20 mm and a 27 mm cannon) and the housing of FuMO 61 air-warning radar antenna are can be seen. (Imperial War Museum)

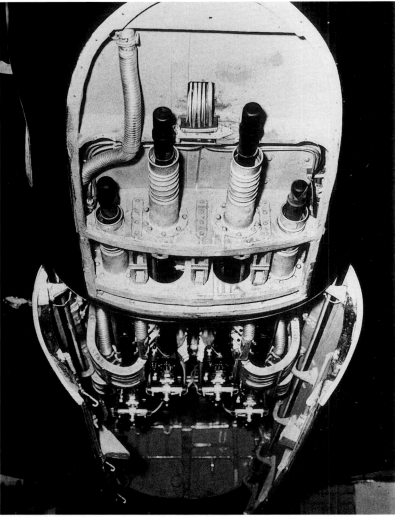

Four Hispano 20 mm cannon in the belly of Mosquito F Mk II. (Hawker Siddeley/British Aerospace)

base in France. On the following day a Whitley from No. 10 Operational Training Unit found the pair, and its depth charges finished off *U564*. The aircraft suffered damage in the encounter, however, and as it was limping home it ran into German fighters and was shot down.

The next two groups of U-boats which attempted to pass through the Bay on the surface set sail on 12 June and had varying fortunes. One, comprising three boats, crossed the Bay without loss after a running fight during which their return fire caused damage to two of the attacking aircraft. The other group, comprising five boats, came under attack from a patrol of Mosquito fighters of No. 307 Squadron which made repeated strafing attacks with cannon. One of the British fighters was damaged, but their cannon shells caused so many casualties on *U68* and *U155* that these boats were forced to return to base.

Following these actions Dönitz made yet another change to his tactics. From 17 June boats were to cross the Bay in groups and would surface only by day, and then only for the minimum time necessary to recharge their batteries—about four hours in each 24. The reduced time on the surface made it much more difficult for patrol aircraft to find the groups and attack them. As a result, during the last two weeks in June, only one U-boat was damaged by air attack in the Bay area.

The German group sailing tactics were not unlike those employed by Allied merchant ships sailing in convoy. And Coastal Command's countertactics bore a striking resemblance to the "Wolf Pack" methods which the U-boats had used with such effect against the Allied convoys. Three times per day a force of seven aircraft would fly on parallel tracks through an

area astride the German transit routes. If a crew encountered a U-boat group, it was to orbit the enemy force and pass details to headquarters, which would order the other aircraft in the "Wolf Pack" to the scene. The aerial "Wolf Pack" tactics were an immediate success, and July 1943 proved to be the most fruitful month of all for patrol aircraft operating over the Bay: 11 U-boats sunk and three seriously damaged, in exchange for six aircraft destroyed by return fire from the submarines.

Each action during this phase had unique features of its own, and none can be described as "typical"; however, the fight on 30 July can be regarded as representative. Early that morning Flying Officer W. Irving and his crew flying a Liberator of No. 53 Squadron sighted a trio of U-boats on the surface: *U461*, *U462*, and *U504* on their way to the Atlantic. The aircraft's radio report to headquarters led to six other aircraft being ordered to the area: a Liberator, two Halifaxes, two Sunderlands, and a Catalina. When the force had assembled, one of the Halifaxes initiated the attack, with a bombing run from 1,600 ft (490 m) during which it released three 600 lb (272 kg) depth bombs (these weapons functioned in the same way as normal depth charges but had stronger cases to suit them for release from higher altitudes). The accurate German anti-aircraft fire inflicted damage on the Halifax; however, its depth bombs fell wide, and it was forced to break off the action. The second Halifax made its attack from 3,000 ft (910 m), where it was somewhat safer from the return fire. One of its depth bombs landed close to *U462* and caused severe damage; the boat slowly lost way and slid to a stop. The other two U-boats circled to provide cover for the crippled craft, and that was the cue for the remaining aircraft to begin a multi-national charge. Irving's Liberator took the lead, accompanied by the other Liberator which belonged to the 19th Antisubmarine Squadron U.S. Army Air Forces; following up behind came the Sunderland which belonged to No. 461 Squadron Royal Australian Air Force. The faster Liberators outpaced the flying boat, but as they ran into attack, they came under concentrated fire, and both suffered minor damage. In the general confusion, however, the Sunderland was able to make its attack run on *U461* almost unnoticed. Only at the last moment did the boat's guns start to traverse in the direction of the flying boat, and by then it was too late; the aircraft's nose gunner had found the range, and his long, accurate burst silenced the U-boat's armament. His target defenseless, the Sunderland pilot was able to release his stick of seven depth charges accurately down the length of the U-boat. Her back broken, the submarine broke in two and sank immediately. At that stage the captain of *U504* decided there was nothing further he could do to help his comrades, and judging that none of the aircraft was in position to make an immediate attack, he took his boat down.

Normally such a move would have enabled *U504* to survive, but while the other aircraft were making their attacks, the Catalina had been directing the five warships of a Royal Navy submarine hunting team to the area. The vessels arrived in time to see the destruction of *U461*, and their gunfire sent *U462* to the bottom shortly afterwards. The warships then carried out a sonar search for *U504* and located and sank her too.

During the first two days in August 1943, Allied patrol aircraft operating over the Bay of Biscay continued in their triumphant vein, sinking four more U-boats. Admiral Dönitz decided that enough was enough. It was clear that the group sailing tactics were not the solution to the problem, and he abandoned their use. He ordered those groups in the outer Bay area to split up and their U-boats to proceed to the west singly, surfacing to recharge their batteries for as short a time as possible *only at night*; he ordered the six boats that had just set out to return. And the four U-boats returning from patrols in the mid-Atlantic, he ordered to hug the Spanish coast without regard for territorial waters, surfacing only at night for the minimum time necessary to recharge the batteries. These tactics were immediately found to be successful, for the general clutter of radar echoes from the land made it very difficult to detect the boats on ASV.

The last of these tactics, hugging the Spanish coast and surfacing only for short periods at night, proved to be the answer to German submariners' problems. Soon afterwards the first boats were equipped with a new type of radar warning receiver, the *Naxos*, which was designed to pick up signals in the 3,000 Megahertz band. From the end of the first week in August until the end of 1943, aircraft patrolling in the Bay area sank only five U-boats and caused damage to one.

The battle of the Bay began early in 1941 and did not finally cease until the German U-boat bases in France were cut off by Allied ground forces in the summer of 1944. But the hardest-fought phase of the battle took place during the 15

months between the early part of June 1942 and the early part of August 1943. During that period aircraft sank a total of 33 German and Italian submarines in the area, they caused serious damage to 30 others, and they shared with surface ships in the destruction of one boat. Unique among the campaigns in which submarines took heavy losses, the Battle of the Bay took place well clear of surface ships the U-boats were trying to attack; in other words, the submarines had been free to choose their tactics, but even so they took a heavy beating from the aircraft.

Above right: The happy homecoming of *U106* at Lorient, France on 22 February 1942. Note the victory pennants beside the attack periscope. (Bundesarchiv) Below: The same boat *U106* under depth charge attack by three Sunderlands of Nos. 228 and 461 (RAAF) Squadrons in the Bay of Biscay on 2 August 1943. (Imperial War Museum)

U185 (Type IXC/40) being sunk after FIDO ("Mark 24 Mine" homing torpedo) attack by an TBF-1 Avenger of VC-13 from USS *Core* (CVE-13) on 24 August 1943. (National Archives)

The Aircraft Triumphant—But Just in Time

Following the defeat of the U-boat packs during the mid-Atlantic convoy battles in May 1943, the German submariners kept clear of that area until September. Then Admiral Dönitz attempted to surprise his enemy with a sudden switch of U-boats back into the area. The German Naval High Command expected much from the *Zaunkönig* homing torpedo which now formed part of each boat's armament; this submarine-launched weapon was similar in concept to the Mark 24 Mine carried by Allied aircraft and was intended for use against the convoy escorts. Forewarned of the return of the U-boats to the mid-Atlantic by information from de-crypted signals, however, the Allied Navies were able to shift forces to meet the renewed threat. Initially the Wolf Packs had some successes, but the familiar pattern returned with boats being lost and fewer sinkings of the convoys. When this series of actions ended in mid-October, the U-boats had sunk a total of eight merchant ships and four escorts, but in achieving that they had lost 12 of their number.

Nor did the renewed German attempt to engage convoys passing through the waters around the Azores, which began in October 1943, yield any better results. Again the U-boats encountered aircraft from American escort carriers,

this time *Card* and *Core*, and four boats were lost to aircraft using the now well-practiced technique of forcing the submarine to dive and then planting a homing torpedo in the diving swirl as it disappeared under the waves.

Following these two rebuffs Admiral Dönitz pulled the bulk of his forces back into port, and there was a further lull in U-boat operations.

Madcats in Action

One German U-boat effort continued throughout this period, however: the sending of boats through the Strait of Gibraltar to reinforce those operating in the Mediterranean. In an attempt to defeat this movement, U.S. Navy VP-63 (Patrol Squadron 63), equipped with PBY-5A Catalina amphibians carrying Magnetic Airborne Detectors and retrobombs, deployed to Port Lyautey in Morocco in January 1944. During February the MAD-fitted Catalinas, nicknamed "Madcats," began flying a barrier patrol over the Strait. Every morning, all morning two aircraft flew round opposite sides of an oblong four miles (7.4 km) long and two miles (3.7 km) wide astride the deep water channel through the Strait. The aircraft completed the orbit once every six minutes and maintained an altitude of 100 ft (30 m) to give their MAD equipment the best chance of detecting any submerged U-boat passing beneath them. At midday a second pair of Madcats would relieve the first and repeat

MAD-fitted PBY-5A Catalina of VPB-63 (redesignated from VP-63 in October 1944) operating over the sea in August 1945. (National Archives)

the performance throughout the afternoon. This attention to procedure brought its reward on 24 February, when one of the Catalinas detected *U761* trying to make her way into the Mediterranean. Both aircraft attacked the boat using 24-bomb patterns of retrobombs; then two Royal Navy destroyers depth charged the badly damaged boat and finished her off. Similar actions on 16 March and 5 May resulted in the destruction of *U392* and *U731*, respectively.

Invasion of Normandy—The Greatest Battle

The early months of 1944 were like a calm before a storm at the German submarine bases on the west coast of France. Few doubted that the long-predicted Allied invasion of western Europe was about to open, and there was considerable speculation on when and where the blow would fall. But one thing was clear: almost all the troops, equipment, and supplies would be transported by sea, and the ships carrying them would provide juicy targets for U-boats. For Germany the course of the war depended on the outcome of the forthcoming battle. Admiral Dönitz was prepared to commit his entire U-boat force and risk heavy losses, if there was a chance of sinking transports carrying the Allied forces.

The Atlantic convoy routes were quiet during the early months of 1944, as Dönitz husbanded his forces and began to assemble as large a force of U-boats as he could in readiness for the decisive battle. He also instituted a crash program to install Schnorkels in as many boats as possible to make them less vulnerable to detection and attack from the air. But despite strenuous efforts by dockyard personnel, the program ran into unexpected difficulties, and the modifications took somewhat longer than expected; moreover, once work on it began the boat was *hors de combat* for several weeks until it was complete. This further reduced the number of submarines ready for action, and at the beginning of June the *Landwirt* Group assembled to counter the Allied invasion comprised less than 50 U-boats. Of these less than ten were fitted with Schnorkel. Though the Group was not as large as the German leaders had hoped, it was still capable of inflicting considerable damage if it could fight its way into the invasion area and engage the transports there.

The Allied planners charged with devising a plan to defeat the expected massed attack by U-boats faced a difficult task. The distance from Brest, the nearest German base, to the main landing area in Normandy was less than 200 miles (370 km); making a high speed dash on the surface, a U-boat could cover most of that distance in a single night. By pulling in aircraft from all other areas, No.19 Group of Coastal Command was reinforced to 23 squadrons of anti-submarine aircraft, comprising some 320 Sunderlands, Wellingtons, Liberators, Halifaxes, and Swordfish flown by British, American, Canadian, Australian, Czech, and Polish crews.

This force was to be employed in flying the appropriately named "Cork" patrols to block the western end of the English Channel. The area of 20,000 square miles (68,600 km²) of sea was divided into 12 adjacent patrol lines, each shaped like an oblong. Once the invasion began, relays of aircraft were simultaneously and continuously to fly around the circumference of every oblong, day and night, so long as the threat of massed attacks by U-boats remained. Every part of the sea area would

Two U.S. Navy Catalinas of VP-63, aided by two Royal Navy destroyers (HMS *Anthony* and *Wishart*), sink *U761* in the Straits of Gibraltar in 24 February 1944. (National Archives)

The Liberator GR Mk IV of No. 220 Squadron, based at Lagens in the Azores, on anti-submarine patrol in Atlantic skies. Note the Leigh Light beneath the starboard wing (Imperial War Museum)

Certainly the plan to prevent U-boats reaching the invasion area looked very effective on paper. But the history of warfare is replete with carefully laid plans which never lived up to the expectations of whose who had drawn them up. Whether this one proved any different would depend on the skill and determination of those charged with carrying it out.

On 6 June 1944 the longest day dawned and the invasion began. At 0513 hours Headquarters German Naval Forces West flashed an order to all U-boats in Group *Landwirt* to come to immediate readiness to put to sea. The most concentrated battle ever between aircraft and submarines was about to open.

At dusk on the evening of the 6th, the *Landwirt* Group, comprising 49 boats, including nine with Schnorkels, set sail from its bases in Western France and headed for the western entrance to the Channel. Those U-boats without Schnorkel had to remain on the surface as long as possible to keep their batteries fully charged for the underwater run when dawn came. As a result they were the first to feel the lash of the "Cork" patrols, which reported 22 contacts leading to seven attacks on U-boats; they sank two boats and damaged five. At dawn the surviving U-boats dived, and the action petered out.

At dusk on 7 June the battle resumed as the 36 U-boats without Schnorkels surfaced and headed for the invasion area at full speed. Shortly after midnight Flying Officer Kenneth Moore RCAF was "pacing his beat" in a Leigh Light Liberator of No.224 Squadron when his radar operator reported a contact 12 miles (22 km) ahead. Skillfully the Canadian pilot side-stepped his aircraft to place the contact between himself and the bright moon, then turned towards it and accelerated to attack speed. A few minutes later his navigator sighted a U-boat against the shimmering line of the moon on the water: "It was a perfect silhouette, as if it were painted on white paper," he later remarked. The Liberator straddled the boat with its six depth charges, and *U629* sank almost immediately. Six minutes later the radar operator reported another contact at a range of six miles (11 km); the second attack was almost a carbon copy of the first, and at the end of it *U373* was on her way to the bottom. Kenneth Moore's achievement—two U-boats sunk in less than half an hour—was unique, and in recognition of it he

thus be swept by radar at least once every 30 minutes. Any U-boat on the surface was liable to be detected with that frequency, but if it dived each time its crew heard enemy radar signals, or lacked a Schnorkel but tried to pass through the area submerged, it would soon end up with flat batteries, unable to dive when the next aircraft approached. As each aircraft reached the end of its allotted time on patrol, another would relieve it; when darkness fell, night-attack aircraft carrying Leigh Lights or flares would take over the patrolling. Reserve aircraft were held on the ground, ready to take off at short notice, to replace aircraft which went unserviceable, expended their weapons, or were shot down. And even if a few U-boats managed to penetrate the 200-mile (370 km) deep thicket of air patrols, they would still have to run the gauntlet of some 300 destroyers, frigates, sloops, corvettes, and anti-submarine trawlers before they could get to the all-important transport ships.

Night picture shows five million candlepower beam of the Leigh Light fitted to the Coastal Command Liberator GR V during an illumination test. (Imperial War Museum)

A Sunderland GR Mk V of No. 201 Squadron patrolling over the sea in 1945. (Imperial War Museum)

was later awarded the Distinguished Service Order.

The hard-fought contest between the U-boats and the "Cork" patrols continued, until by dawn on the 10th the aircraft had sunk six boats and damaged six more: almost one-quarter of the entire *Landwirt* Group. Despite these painful losses no boat without Schnorkel had succeeded in getting any closer to the invasion area than the Channel Islands. By 12 June it was clear to the German Naval High Command that the air patrols had got the best of the contest, and the 22 surviving U-boats without Schnorkel were ordered to return to base. As they extricated themselves from the air patrols, one more boat was sunk, and five were damaged.

That still left the Schnorkel-fitted boats, of which six of the original nine were still trying to pick their way through to air and sea patrols guarding the transports. Only on 15 June, nine days after the Allied landings began, did the first of these reach the invasion area; it sank an American tank-landing ship before surface-hunting teams hounded it out of the area. A fortnight would pass before the second German boat reached that rich if hazardous hunting ground, but by then the critical period for the landings had passed, and the Allied beachhead was secure. Harassed to the point of exhaustion by the Allied air and sea patrols, the U-boats of the *Landwirt* Group had been unable to exert any real influence on the decisive battle for the beaches.

The first air attack on a Schnorkeling U-boat took place on 18 June, when one of the crew of a Liberator of U.S. Navy VP-110 (Patrol Squadron 110) caught sight of the breathing tube of *U275* protruding above the surface as she was rumbling through the English Channel; the subsequent depth-charge attack caused minor damage to the boat. Just over three weeks elapsed before there was a similar sighting, but on that occasion a Sunderland of No. 201 Squadron sank *U1222*. These encounters showed that boats running on Schnorkel were liable to be detected visually, but unless the sea was calm the chances of doing so were remote.

During 1944 the Coastal Command tactical development team had put together a procedure for attacking submerged submarines in open water, using a combination of sonobuoys and homing torpedoes. The method was not reliable and depended for its success on considerable skill from the crew of the aircraft, plus a measure of luck. Because of this several months would pass before the use of the technique secured the destruction of a U-boat. On 20 March 1945 Flight Lieutenant N. Smith and his crew, flying a Liberator of No.86 Squadron, were on patrol over an area of known U-boat activity off the Orkney Islands when the radar operator reported a suspicious contact three miles (5.6 km) away. The Liberator closed on the object, but it disappeared into sea clutter on the radar at half a mile (930 m). By then it was almost dark, the aircraft carried neither a Leigh Light nor flares, and the lookouts could see no sign of the object. Two further runs over the area failed to secure a sighting on the mystery object which at this stage did not justify an attack: it could well have been a piece of flotsam. Smith's suspicions were aroused, however, so he decided to lay down a pattern of sonobuoys: one buoy at the center, followed by four more 2 1/4 miles (4.2 km) from it laid out in the form of a square.

Mosquito FB IV fighter-bombers of No. 143 Squadron attack on two U-boats with 3 in AP rockets in Kattegat on 2 May, 1945. (British Aerospace)

As the first sonobuoy came on the air, the operator heard the unmistakable swish of a propeller thrashing at 114 rpm—a U-boat. One by one the other sonobuoys switched themselves on, and the operator was able to narrow the position of the boat to one part of the pattern. While he was doing so the radar operator caught a further short glimpse of the object he had first seen; now there was no doubt that it was a Schnorkel head. With the target identified and located sufficiently for his purpose, Smith pulled the Liberator on to an attack heading. With the navigator counting off the seconds, the aircraft flew a timed run along the bearing of the final radar contact. Over the position where the navigator computed the boat to be, Smith released his two homing torpedoes. Throughout this painstaking activity overhead, the unsuspecting U-boat had been cruising purposefully towards its operating area, and it would be allowed to continue to do so for a little longer: it took six minutes for the first homing torpedo to catch up with the boat. Then the sonobuoy operator heard a long reverberating sound in his phones, after which there were only sea noises. There was no other evidence that the attack had been successful, but post-war examination of German records revealed that *U905* had disappeared without trace in that area at about the time of Smith's attack.

The Final Months

Following the end of the battle around the invasion area, there was virtual stalemate in the U-boat war around the coast of Europe and in the Atlantic. Now boats made infrequent sorties and usually operated singly, for Admiral Dönitz's aim was to exert only sufficient pressure to force the Allies to maintain the huge forces of aircraft and warships devoted to anti-submarine operations. For his part he needed to preserve his experienced men to ensure there would be sufficient crews to man the new types of U-boat being launched in ever-increasing numbers.

In mid-1944 the first Type XXIII boats were accepted by the German Navy, and crews began training to handle the new craft in the quiet waters of the Baltic. It was January 1945 before the first Type XXIII was ready for an operational sortie, however. Between then and the end of the war, five of these boats saw action in the waters around the British Isles and sank six ships without loss to themselves. The boats operated in areas where there were intense air patrols which, thanks to the information from de-crypted signals, were centered on the very areas where the boats were known to be. But in spite of this, the new type of U-boat, with its enlarged battery capacity and Schnorkel, was able to operate in these areas with near-impunity. The success of the Type XXIII provides a clear indication of what the much larger and more powerful Type XXI boat might have achieved, but the war ended before either it or the hydrogen-peroxide powered Type XVII could go into action. So far as the Allied anti-submarine forces were concerned, the war against Germany came to an end in the nick of time.

Type XXI U-boat

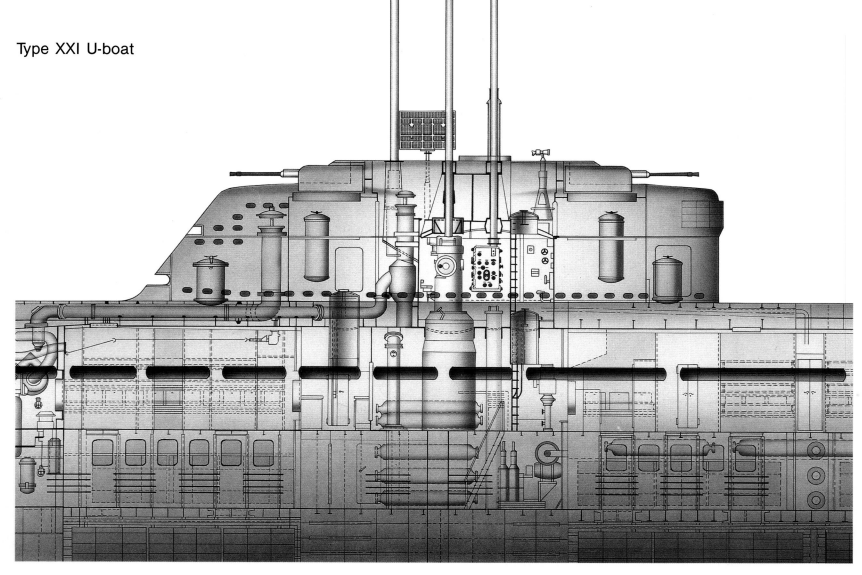

A Mitsubishi Type 0 Mk 11 observation seaplane (F1M2, Pete) of the 19th *Kokutai* (Air Group), armed with two 60 kg (132 lb) bombs takes off from the base at Jaluit Island in the Central Pacific, 1942. (Yōji Watanabe)

The Hokuto *Kokutai's* Nakajima Type 97 Mk 12 torpedo-bomber (B5N2, Kate), loaded with a 250 kg (551 lb) anti-submarine bomb, going to daily patrol flight from Kataoka naval base in Northern Kurile Islands, April 1945. (Yukitaka Noguchi)

The War in the Pacific

Operations by U.S. and Allied Submarines in the Pacific

Of the Axis powers only Japan depended on raw materials from overseas and was therefore forced to rely on shipping routes that were vulnerable to submarine attack. That nation produced neither cotton nor wool, rubber, or bauxite (aluminium ore), and she had no indigenous oil; she produced only a quarter of the iron ore she used, a third of the wood pulp, and half the industrial salt. As the nation moved on to a war footing, the need to step up shipments of these raw materials imposed a severe strain on the Japanese merchant marine, which was scarcely large enough for the task even at the beginning.

At the start of the war in the Pacific, the U.S. and Dutch Navies had a total of 62 submarines available for operations. During the initial Allied retreat these forces were mainly engaged in defensive operations; but as the battle fronts stabilized these boats, assisted by a few from the Royal Navy, began to take a steady toll of Japanese merchant shipping. In this task the Allied submariners were greatly assisted by two important factors. First, the Japanese had been dilatory in enforcing the convoy system, and not until January 1944 was this in general use. Secondly, there was a wealth of intelligence from de-crypted Japanese signals, for these were being read with the same facili-

ty as those of the German Navy. As a result Allied boats were frequently positioned off ports or in narrow straits through which enemy shipping was passing, and since few of the ships had escorts, the boats could close in and use their weapons to greatest effect. The steady war of attrition brought about a severe depletion of the Japanese merchant marine, and by the beginning of 1944 it had lost about half its pre-war tonnage of ships. Even with the inclusion of new, captured, and salvaged ships, the size of the fleet had been reduced by one-quarter.

In November 1943 the Japanese Navy made a tardy attempt to reduce this debilitating loss rate with the formation of the General Escort Command under Admiral Koshiro Oikawa, responsible for that Navy's overall anti-submarine effort. Yet while the idea was good, its execution was poor, and the Japanese Navy regarded the Command as a second-rate force charged with carrying out a mission of secondary importance. Oikawa was given control of four escort carriers, the *Taiyo*, the *Unyo*, the *Shinyo*, and the *Kaiyo*, and some 250 aircraft, most of which were obsolescent types such as the Nakajima B5N (Allied code-name Kate) and the Aichi D3A (Val) single-engined carrier based bombers, and Aichi E13A (Allied code-name Jake) and Mitsubishi F1M (Pete) single-engined floatplanes. Gradually this force expanded and improved in quality, until by May 1945 there were some 450 aircraft of all types, including Mitsubishi G3M (Nell) and G4M (Betty) twin-engined bombers,

U.S. Navy submarine *Redfish* (SS-395) immediately after surfacing on 15 February 1945. *Redfish* sank the Japanese carrier *Unryu* in the East China Sea on 19 December 1944. (National Archives)

A line-up of Kyushu *Tokai* Mk 11 (Q1W1, Lorna) patrol aircraft of the 901st *Kokutai*, General Escort Command, at the 2nd Chitose air base in Hokkaido after the end of the war. Note Type 3 Air Model 6 radar antennas on the nearest aircraft. (Smithsonian Institution)

and Kawanishi H6K (Mavis) and H8K (Emily) four-engined flying boats. Yet despite the shortage of modern equipment it provided for its anti-submarine force, the Japanese Navy was the only service taking part in the conflict to operate an aircraft purpose-designed for the anti-submarine role: the Kyushu Q1W *Tokai* (Lorna), a small twin-engined machine with a crew of three, a maximum speed of 174 knots (200 mph, 322 km/h), a range of 725 miles (1,340 km), and able to carry 500 kg (1,102 lb) of anti-submarine bombs. This type saw service in small numbers during the closing stages of the war.

Compared with those of the western Allies, the submarine-detection devices and weapons fitted to the Japanese aircraft were crude and inefficient. Only in mid-1943 did an airborne radar become available, but the set, the Navy Type 3 Air Model 6, was similar in capability to the ASV Mark II equipment then being replaced by newer centimetric wavelength equipment on Allied patrol aircraft. The Japanese Navy also in-

troduced the Type 3 Model 1 *Jiki-Tanchiki* (KMX) magnetic airborne detector, a device similar in performance to its American counterpart. There was no Japanese equivalent of the Leigh Light. Some of their anti-submarine planes carried high intensity flares, but for the most part the crews lacked the specialized training necessary to press home effective attacks at night. In any case the U.S. submarines' APR-1 and SPR-1 warning receivers usually picked up signals from the enemy radar in time to dive before an attack could develop.

The main anti-submarine weapons carried by Japanese aircraft were anti-submarine bombs and small general-purpose bombs. There was no equivalent to the retrobomb for use with magnetic detection equipment, nor anything comparable with the "Mark 24 Mine" homing torpedo.

The records of the General Escort Command for 27 August 1944 gave an insight into its operational methods:

"A magnetic detector aircraft of the Manila detach-

Aichi Type 0 Mk 11b Reconnaissance Seaplane (E13A1b, Allied Code name: Jake)

Power unit
Mitsubishi *Kinsei* Mk 43 14-cylinder air-cooled engine:
   1,060 hp for take-off
   1,080 hp at 2,000 m (6,560 ft)
Dimensions
Span: 14.50 m (47 ft 6⁷/₈ in)
Span, wings folded: 7.413 m (24 ft 3⁷/₈ in)
Length, level position: 11.265 m (36 ft 11½ in)
Height, level position: 4.70 m (15 ft 5 in)
Wing area: 39.67 m² (427 sq ft)
Weights, without MAD
Empty: 2,642 kg (5,825 lb)
Gross: 3,650 kg (8,050 lb)
Performance
Max speed: 376 km/h (234 mph) at 2,180 m (7,150 ft)
Cruising speed: 222 km/h (138 mph) at 2,000 m (6,560 ft)
Time to climb to 5,000 m (16,400 ft): 8 min 32 sec
Service ceiling: 8,730 m (28,640 ft)
Range: 2,090 km (1,300 mls)
Armament
1 × 7.7 mm Type 92 flexible mounted machine gun
1 × 250 kg (551 lb) or 4 × 60 kg (132 lb) bombs
Anti-submarine equipment
Type 3 Model 1 magnetic airborne detector (KMX)
Crew 3

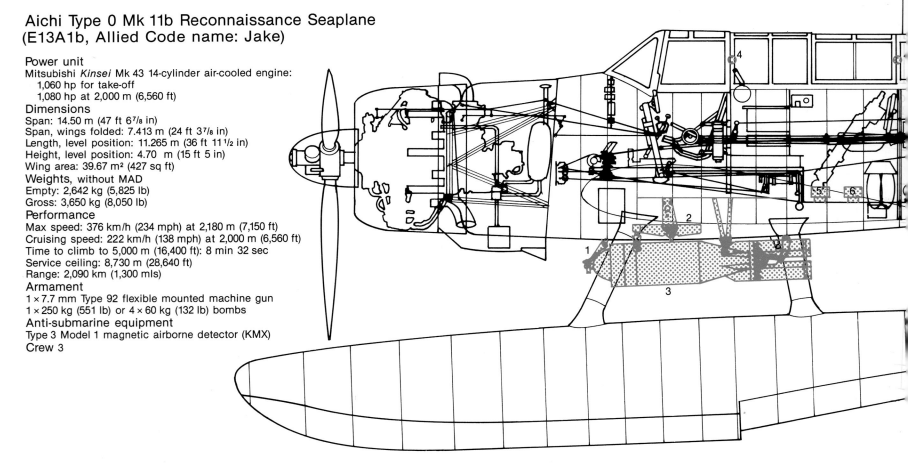

A Kawanishi Type 97 Mk 22 Flying boat (H6K4, Mavis) in service with the 901st *Kokutai*, General Escort Command, gets airborne for long-range patrol in the summer of 1944.
(Yoji Watanabe)

**Japanese Navy 250 kg (551 lb)
Type 1 No. 25 Model 2
anti-submarine bomb**

Overall length: 1,910 mm (6 ft 3³⁄₁₆ in)
Body diameter: 357 mm (1 ft 2¹⁄₁₆ in)
Wall thickness: 10 mm (³⁄₈ in)
Total weight: 266 kg (586 lb)
Weight of filling: 144 kg (317 lb)
Effective range: 20 m (65 ft)

1. Ring struts
2. Playwood extension tail fins
3. Vanes
4. Fuze
5. Light sheet-metal tail fins
6. Explosive cavity
7. Suspension lug
8. Anti-ricochet nose ring
9. Exploder

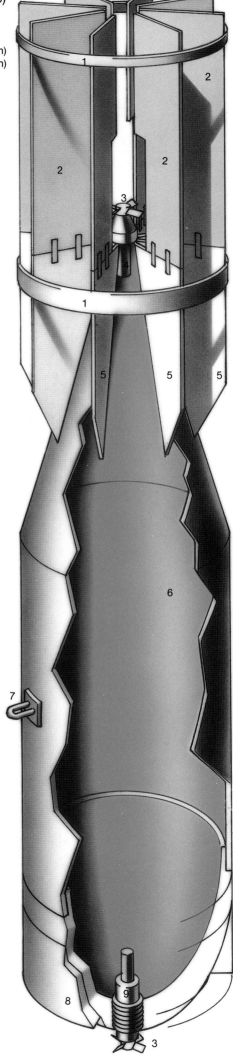

ment of the 901st Air Group found a submarine at 0916 on the 27th at 16° 28′N, 119° 44′E [off the west of Luzon in the Philippines]. Bombed with two 250 kg (551 lb) bombs, result unknown. Then at 0935 another magnetic detector aircraft found a submarine near the previous position and cooperated with seven medium bombers, some floatplanes of the 954th Air Group, and some Army planes to bomb it. The following day an aircraft observed an oil slick 10 km (5.4 miles) long and 4 km (2.2 miles) wide in the same area, and so confirmed [sic] that the submarine had been destroyed."

Although an oil slick *might* indicate that a submarine had been sunk, by itself it does not constitute proof; U.S. Navy records mention no submarine loss that can be attributed to the attacks described above.

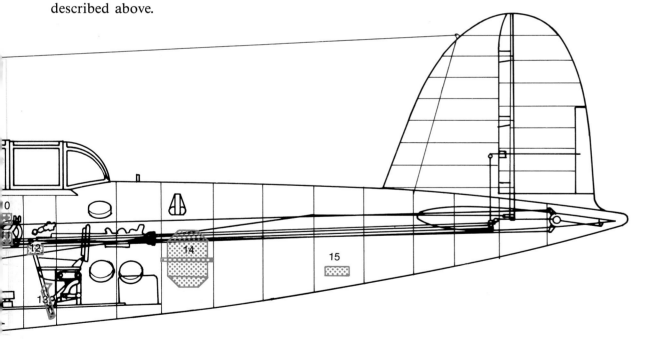

1. Vane stoppers
2. Pylon
3. 250 kg (551 lb) Type 1 No. 25 Model 2 anti-submarine bomb
4. Buzzers
5. Generator
6. Alternating current transformer
7. Signal display control
8. Direct current amplifier
9. Signal frequency selector
10. Marker release control
11. Switch box
12. Noise eliminate coil regulator
13. Automatic signal flare shooter
14. Magnetic detector (gyro-stabilized coil) container
15. Noise eliminate coil
    (4–15: parts of Type 3 Model 1 magnetic airborne detector)

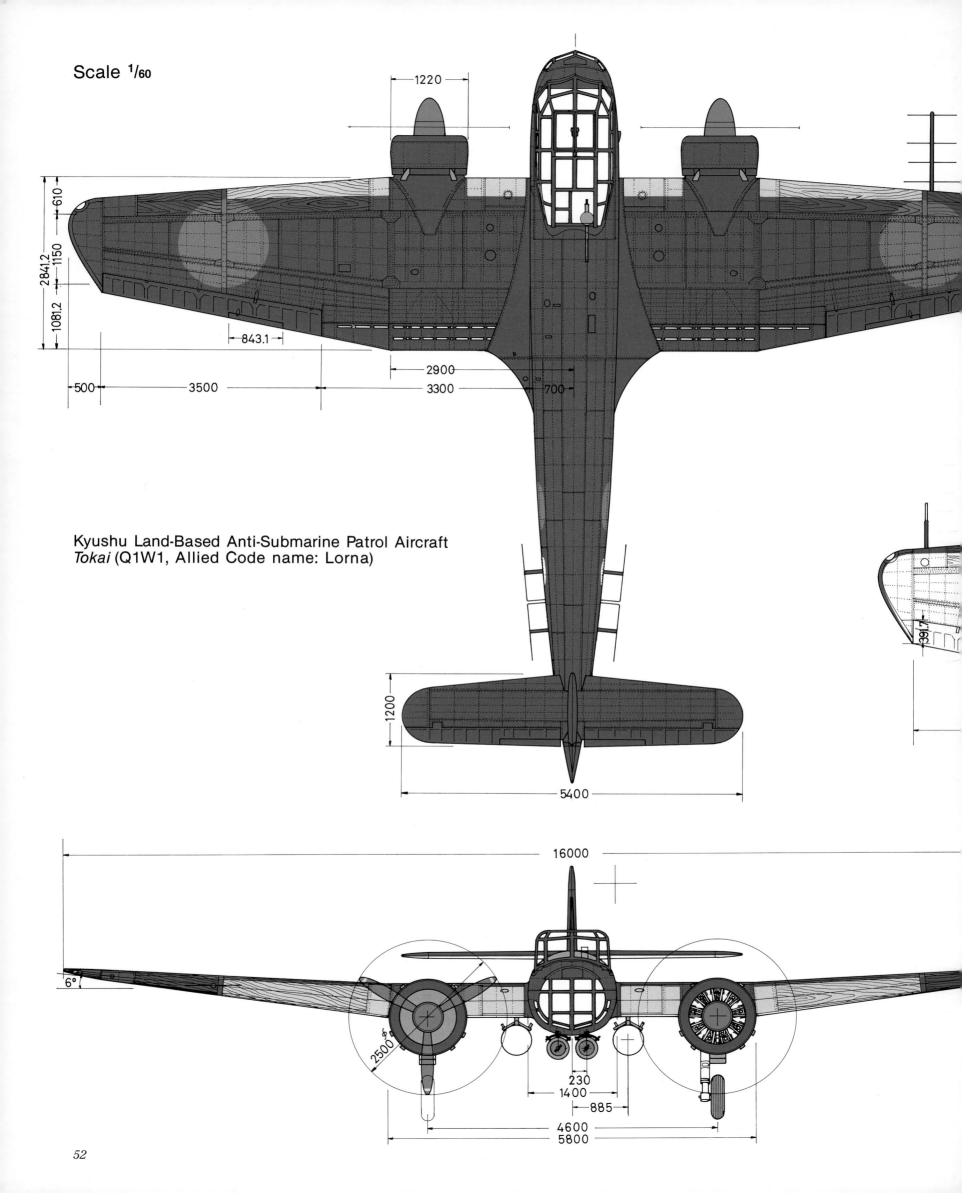

Scale $^1/_{60}$

Kyushu Land-Based Anti-Submarine Patrol Aircraft
Tokai (Q1W1, Allied Code name: Lorna)

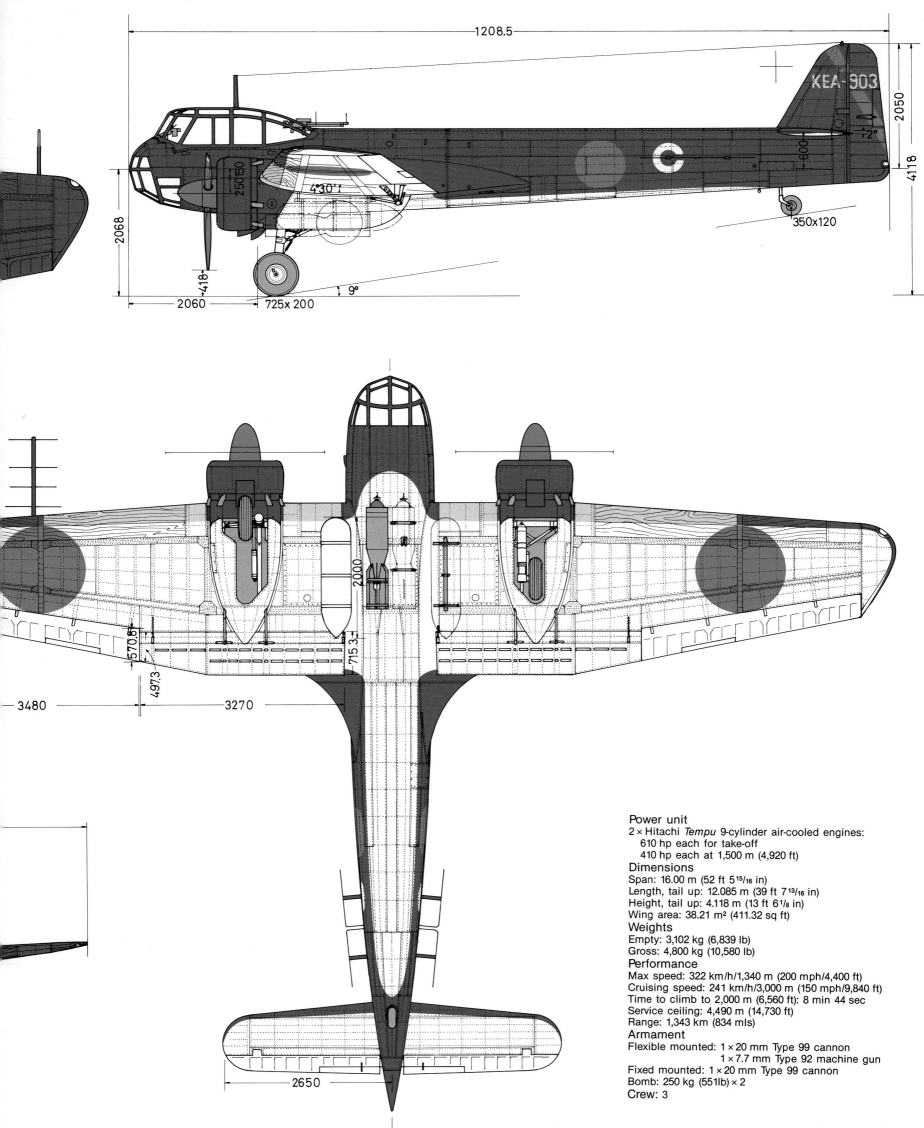

Power unit
2 × Hitachi *Tempu* 9-cylinder air-cooled engines:
  610 hp each for take-off
  410 hp each at 1,500 m (4,920 ft)
Dimensions
Span: 16.00 m (52 ft 5^{15}/$_{16}$ in)
Length, tail up: 12.085 m (39 ft 7^{13}/$_{16}$ in)
Height, tail up: 4.118 m (13 ft 6^{1}/$_{8}$ in)
Wing area: 38.21 m² (411.32 sq ft)
Weights
Empty: 3,102 kg (6,839 lb)
Gross: 4,800 kg (10,580 lb)
Performance
Max speed: 322 km/h/1,340 m (200 mph/4,400 ft)
Cruising speed: 241 km/h/3,000 m (150 mph/9,840 ft)
Time to climb to 2,000 m (6,560 ft): 8 min 44 sec
Service ceiling: 4,490 m (14,730 ft)
Range: 1,343 km (834 mls)
Armament
Flexible mounted: 1 × 20 mm Type 99 cannon
                 1 × 7.7 mm Type 92 machine gun
Fixed mounted: 1 × 20 mm Type 99 cannon
Bomb: 250 kg (551lb) × 2
Crew: 3

Generally there was only poor coordination when Japanese ships and aircraft attempted to engage enemy submarines. One of the few occasions when the system worked effectively was on 14 November 1944, after USS *Halibut* attacked a convoy off Formosa. A *Jiki-Tanchiki* aircraft located her and dropped markers; then two of the surface escorts launched a vigorous counter-attack which damaged the submarine to such an extent that she was lucky to escape.

With so much going against it, there was little the General Escort Command could do to stave off disaster from the steadily growing U.S. submarine fleet exploiting the intelligence derived from de-crypted signals. In the course of 1944 the Japanese merchant marine lost 3,820,000 tons of shipping from all causes, more than during the previous two years put together; at the end of the year only 2,850,000 tons remained. Nor could the General Escort Command deploy forces with impunity. During the summer and autumn of 1944, U.S. submarines torpedoed and sank three of the four escort carriers and several escorts assigned to the Command.

Typical of the one-sided actions which often resulted when U.S. boats pressed home attacks was that fought around Convoy Hi 71 in August. Initially the convoy comprised 18 large merchantmen, a naval oiler, and a transport, with a covering force of seven escorts and the carrier *Taiyo*. Hi 71 left Moji in the west of Japan on 8 August, bound for Singapore. The convoy reached Macao without incident, where five of the merchantmen left and one merchantman and five more escorts joined it. Thus reconstituted, Hi 71 set sail from Macao on the 17th. On the following day a U.S. submarine attacked and damaged one of the merchantmen, which limped away to Formosa escorted by a warship. That evening the convoy ran into bad weather off the Philippine Islands which forced the ships to break formation. USS *Rasher* was able to close on the escort carrier *Taiyo* and sank her with torpedoes; during the small hours of the following morning, the same submarine went on to sink three merchantmen and the oiler, and damage two merchantmen, before breaking off the engagement. After daybreak three of the escorts left the convoy to conduct an unsuccessful anti-submarine sweep in the area where the ships had gone down, but on their way to Manila afterwards, they came under

attack from the submarines *Harder* and *Haddo*, and all three escorts went to the bottom. Re-formed in Manila with 12 merchant ships and 6 escorts, Hi 71 left the port on 26 August and reached Singapore without further loss on 1 September.

By the end of 1944 Japanese convoys on the west Pacific routes were liable to attack not only from enemy submarines but also from aircraft operating from carriers or newly acquired land bases. In the face of this multiple onslaught, there were occasions when the convoys were wiped out altogether. For example, on the last day of December 1944, a convoy of seven tankers and seven cargo ships, protected by eight escorts, left Japan for Sumatra sailing via Formosa, Saigon, and Singapore. As the convoy neared Formosa U.S. submarines sank four of the ships, and while the ships were in harbor they were attacked by U.S. bombers which sank four more. Soon after the convoy left Formosa, one of the escorts suffered a mechanical breakdown and had to return to port. Then the approach of a U.S. Navy carrier task force forced the convoy to make a hasty dash for Hong Kong; it was there when aircraft attacked the port and sank four of its merchantmen and three escorts, and damaged a cargo ship so severely that she could not continue the voyage. The sole surviving merchantman, the tanker *Sarawak Maru*, ar-

A Type 0 Mk 11a reconnaissance seaplane (E13A1a, Jake) of the 902nd *Kokutai* at Truk Islands in the Central Pacific, 1944. (National Archives)

USS *Gudgeon* (SS-211, photographed in August 1943) was sunk by Japanese aircraft in the Philippine Sea on 16 April 1944. (National Archives)

The Douglas SBD-6 Dauntless loaded with a 350 lb (160 kg) depth charge on anti-submarine patrol, 12 November 1943. The battleship *Washington* (BB-56) and the fast carrier *Lexington* (CV-16), part of TF 50, on the way to raid the Gilbert Islands. (National Archives)

rived off Singapore—its penultimate port of call—on 24 January after 25 days in transit. As she was passing through one of the channels leading to the harbor she set off an air-dropped mine which caused such serious damage that she had to be beached. The rough handling suffered by this and other convoys forced the Japanese Navy to cease sailings of merchant ships between Japan and Malaya and the Dutch East Indies after March 1945.

When the Pacific War came to an end in August 1945, the Japanese merchant marine possessed only one-third the tonnage it had had at the beginning of the war. Most of the losses, amounting to 1,150 ships of 500 tons or larger, had been sunk by enemy submarines. It was a chilling pointer to what might have happened in the Atlantic had the Allies not developed powerful anti-submarine forces and successfully broken into the German U-boat cipher system. Of the 288 American submarines sent into action, 52 were lost, 41 of which were sunk by Japanese forces. Of that 41, four U.S. boats are believed to have

been destroyed by Japanese aircraft and 11 more by ships assisted by aircraft.

Operations by Japanese Submarines

Compared with that of its German ally, the Japanese submarine force achieved little during the three and a half years of the war in the Pacific. Japanese submarines were used mainly to attack warships or as scouts for the surface battle fleet, rather than against convoys of merchantmen sailing through that area.

The first Japanese submarine sunk from the air was the *I-170*, which was dive bombed by a Dauntless aircraft from the carrier *Enterprise* on 10 December 1941 and sent to the bottom. During the years that followed Allied anti-submarine units operating in the Pacific theater were greatly strengthened by the introduction of detection equipment and weapons similar to those being used in the Atlantic. But the Japanese boats avoided convoys and other intensively patrolled areas, and as a result, they rarely encountered enemy aircraft. Between January 1942

A Type 97 flying boat is being attached to *I-122* for refueling, fifteen-months before the outbreak of war. The *I-122* was sunk by the American submarine *Skate* (SS-305) on 10 April 1945. (Yoji Watanabe)

Depth charges-fitted Curtiss SB2C-3 Helldiver of VB-18, swings in for landing aboard her carrier *Intrepid* (CV-11) after the anti-submarine patrol on 12 August 1944. (National Archives)

A Vought OS2U Kingfisher, loaded with depth charges, taxies in a strong wind at east-coast base after patrol duty over the Atlantic. (National Archives)

and the end of 1944, U.S. aircraft sank only two Japanese submarines in the Pacific and assisted surface ships to sink a few more.

Between January 1945 and the end of the war in August, U.S. Navy patrol aircraft encountered enemy submarines rather more frequently than had been the case in previous years. During April and May aircraft from the escort carrier *Anzio* sank two boats, and those from *Bataan* assisted by surface ships sank one more. Altogether aircraft sank six Japanese boats and assisted surface ships to destroy one more during the eight-month period; even so, the anti-submarine activity in that theater was on a relatively small scale, and there was none of the technical and tactical thrust-and-parry that took place during the Battle of the Atlantic.

The Maritime Patrol Aircraft Versus the Submarine During World War II

During the six years of war between 1939 and 1945, the anti-submarine aircraft had evolved from a short-ranged, short-sighted, poorly armed daylight attack vehicle into a proven killer which held dominion over the surface of even the

remotest areas of sea by day and by night—and woe betide the submarine crew that dared to dispute the fact.

Yet the submarine had also evolved during the conflict, and by the end of it there existed boats which could operate effectively without ever having to surface fully: the day of the *true* submarine had dawned. Cruising on Schnorkel in open and wind-tossed seas, these boats were virtually immune to radar detection even from aircraft fitted with the best equipment in service in 1945. Trials carried out by the Royal Air Force showed that such a search was only about *six* per cent efficient; that is to say, for every six Schnorkel heads that were detected on radar, a further 94 had come within range of the equipment but had passed unnoticed against the general clutter of echoes from the sea itself. Thus by 1945 the wheel of fortune for the maritime patrol aircraft had gone full circle; having evolved from a blunt and ineffectual weapon into a deadly killer of submarines, by the end of the war the latest anti-submarine aircraft were little more capable than their 1939 predecessors vis-à-vis the latest types of submarine. The large-battery-capacity Schnorkel submarine emerged from the Second World War technically, though not militarily, triumphant.

The Boeing Fortress GR Mk IIA of No. 220 Squadron and crewmen belonged to RAF Coastal Command. Antennas of ASV Mk II radar, one of the most effective equipments for U-boat hunting, are visible on the nose and beneath the port wing. (Imperial War Museum)

The last of twenty Consolidated Liberator Mk Is, AM929, crosses the Atlantic for service with RAF. (Imperial War Museum)

Appendix

Liberator AM929: Sub-Hunting Aircraft Supreme

Liberator AM929 was rolled out of the Consolidated Corporation's plant at San Diego, California, in May 1941. After flight testing at La Guardia and Wright Field, the aircraft was formally handed over to its customer, the British Purchasing Commission to the USA. A Royal Air Force ferry crew collected the bomber and flew her across the Atlantic, arriving at Prestwick in Scotland on 20 August.

Following initial modification work by the Scottish Aviation Company at Prestwick, AM929 flew to the RAF test establishment at Boscombe Down for performance trials. In January 1942 the aircraft returned to Scottish Aviation where she received the full program of modifications to prepare her for the maritime patrol role; as well as British-type bomb racks for up to eight 250 lb (113 kg) depth charges, these included the fitting of ASV Mark II radar, the installation of a large blister under the fuselage containing four 20 mm cannon fixed to fire forwards, hand-held machine guns in defensive positions in the beam and tail, and a maritime color scheme of white overall except for the top surfaces. Equipment shortages delayed the conversion, and it was late in July 1942 before the work was complete.

At the beginning of August AM929 was delivered to No. 120 Squadron, then re-forming with Liberators at Ballykelly in Northern Ireland. On arrival the aircraft had the squadron identification OH painted in large black letters aft of the fuselage roundel and the individual letter H forward of it. Thus AM929 became known affectionately to those who flew in her as H-How.

The start of H-How's operational career was inauspicious. Her first sortie, a 15-hour convoy escort mission over the mid-Atlantic

on 9 August, passed off without incident. And the next two operational sorties had to be terminated early, the first by a fuel leak and the second by engine trouble.

Following this poor start the Liberator's fortunes picked up. While on patrol over the mid-Atlantic on 19 August, her crew located and attacked a U-boat on the surface near the westbound convoy SL118; at the time it was thought the boat had suffered damage, but later examination of German records would show this had not been the case. Shortly afterwards H-How came upon another U-boat on the surface, which was strafed with cannon. Although both U-boats escaped serious damage, they were forced to dive and so lost contact with the convoy they were about to attack.

In September 1942 H-How formed part of a detachment from No. 120 Squadron which operated from Reykjavik, Iceland, in support of a series of convoys carrying supplies round the north of Norway to Russia. The Liberator flew several sorties, and on three occasions her crews sighted U-boats; each time the submarine was able to dive to safety before it could be attacked, but the act of doing so forced it to lose contact with the convoy. Also during these operations H-How drove off a German long-range patrol aircraft, probably a Focke-Wulf Condor, which had been shadowing a convoy; it would be the Liberator's first and only meeting with an enemy aircraft.

In October H-How returned to Ballykelly to resume operations over the mid-Atlantic, and on the 12th she was the mount for Squadron Leader Terrence Bulloch and his crew when they sank *U597*.

On H-How's next sortie, three days later, Flying Officer 'Red' Esler was at the controls, and again the Liberator saw action. The crew sighted two U-boats on the surface near the eastbound convoy SL-104. Esler strafed the first with cannon, then attacked the second with depth charges as it was diving. There was no visible result. Later that day Esler attacked a third U-boat with his remaining depth charges, again seemingly without result. Only on post-war examination of German records did it become clear that *U661* had gone down with all hands in that area on that day after being attacked from the air, and the loss did not link with any other attack.

On 16 October H-How again saw action, for the third time in three sorties, but on that occasion the U-boat escaped without damage. There followed two uneventful sorties, then a sortie during which her crew sighted three boats and launched an unsuccessful attack on one of them.

H-How's run of kills resumed. On 5 November Terrence Bulloch was at the controls of the Liberator escorting the eastbound convoy SL107. Once again her crew sighted a trio of U-boats on the surface closing in to attack the ships. Bulloch singled out one of the boats, dived to attack it, and released the depth charges from low altitude. When the plumes of spray subsided, the stern of a submarine was seen protruding from the water. Then slowly it sank out of sight in a large patch of bubbles, the last that was ever seen of *U132*. During the same patrol Bulloch attacked another U-boat with his remaining depth charges but failed to inflict serious damage.

During December H-How attacked two further U-boats without causing damage; then in January 1943 she went to Canada for a major overhaul and the fitting of replacement engines.

Early in April 1943 the work was complete, and H-How resumed operations with No. 120 Squadron which was now operating from Reykjavik. During the ten weeks that followed the overhaul, the Liberator seemed to be dogged by bad luck. On 5 April a periscope was sighted, but it disappeared before the crew could attack; and on the 22nd her crew sighted no fewer than four U-boats, but each time they ran in to attack, the depth charges failed to release. During the following two months the Liberator flew nine sorties, all of which were uneventful.

For H-How the period of calm ceased on 24 June 1943, when Pilot Officer A. Fraser and his crew took her on a sortie that proved all too eventful. On their way to join westbound convoy ONS11, the crew sighted a fully surfaced U-boat. The German lookouts were alert, however, and as the Liberator dived in to attack, the boat's gunners replied with vigorous defensive fire. One of their cannon shells exploded in the aircraft's nose compartment, causing splinter wounds to the flight engineer and wrecking the hydraulic system. Deprived of hydraulic power the bomb doors began to inch closed, with the result that when the pilot pressed the button to release the depth charges only two fell clear of the aircraft. But they would be sufficient. Both exploded alongside the conning tower, and when the plumes of water subsided, the bow of the U-boat rose steeply from the water, then slid out of sight. *U194* was on the way to her final resting place.

After the attack H-How's crew took stock of their situation, and it became clear the damage was more serious than they had thought. As well as the damage to the nose, a cannon shell had exploded in the port wing outboard of the engine and left a large hole, and the starboard fuel tanks had been punctured and were leaking. One of the crew cranked open the bomb doors using the emergency handle, then Fraser jettisoned the remaining depth charges and began the long flight back to Reykjavik.

When they arrived over their base, the crew used the emergency systems to lower the flaps and undercarriage. But the Liberator's brakes were out of action, and the nosewheel could neither be steered nor locked straight. To prevent the aircraft swinging off the runway after touchdown Frazer decided he would land it tail-down, so he ordered most of the crew to move to the rear fuselage carrying the ammunition belts and other items equipment to get the center of gravity well aft.

The pilot then made a perfect approach and a very slow three-point landing. On touch-down he told the co-pilot to cut the two inboard engines, leaving the outboard engines throttled back but ready

Consolidated Liberator Mk I (LB-30B or "B-24A Conversion") of No. 120 Squadron, flown by Squadron Leader Terrence Bulloch.

for use in case a swing developed. After a ground roll of about 1,000 yards (910 m), the aircraft started to swing to port, but Frazer increased power on that side and held the machine straight; the Liberator came to rest on the runway with only minor skin damage to the underside of the rear fuselage.

Within a month the damage was repaired, and H-How went back in action, but there was little U-boat activity around the convoys in the mid-Atlantic in August and September 1943, and those flying her sighted no U-boats. Then, on 17 October while operating south of Greenland, H-How and a Liberator from another squadron caught an enemy submarine on the surface. Both carried out attacks, which resulted in the destruction of *U540*.

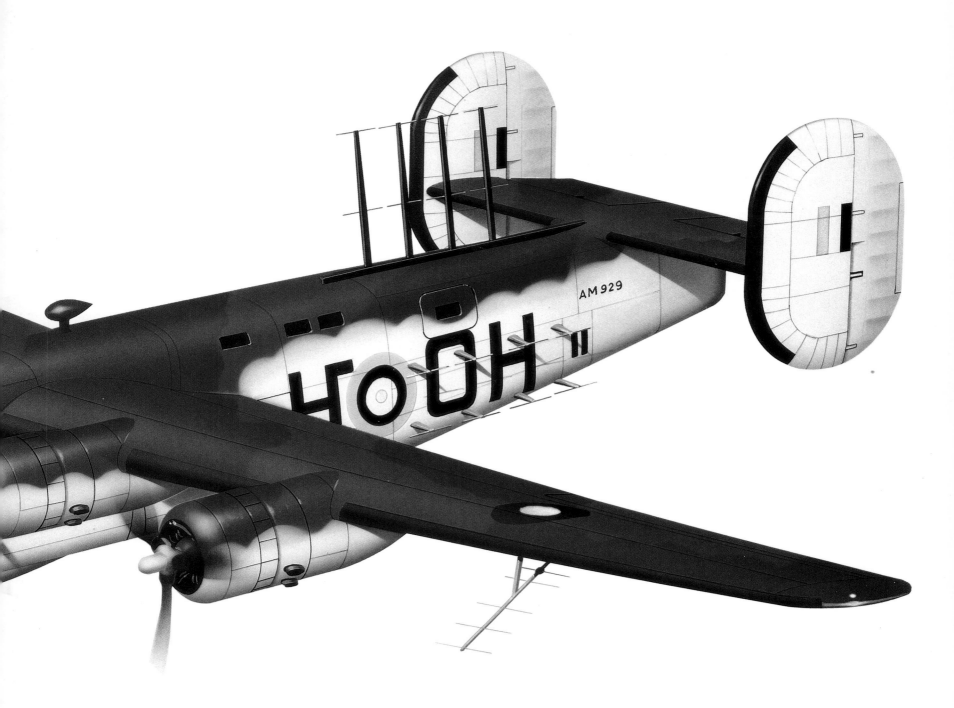

Power unit
4 × Pratt & Whitney R-1830-33 14-cylinder air-cooled engines:
   1,200 hp each for take-off
   1,000 hp each at 14,500 ft (4,420 m)
Dimensions
Span: 110 ft 0 in (33.53 m)
Length, on the ground: 63 ft 9 in (19.43 m)
Height, on the ground: 18 ft 8 in (5.69 m)
Wing area: 1,048 sq ft (97.36 m²)
Weights (B-24A)
Empty: 30,000 lb (13,610 kg)
Gross: 39,350 lb (17,850 kg)

Performance (B-24A)
Max speed: 292.5 mph (471 km/h) at 15,000 ft (4,570 m)
Cruising speed: 228 mph (367 km/h)
Time to climb to 10,000 ft (3,050 m): 5 min 36 sec
Service ceiling: 30,500 ft (9,300 m)
Range with 4,000 lb (1,815 kg) bombs:2,200 mls (3,540 km)
Armament
Fixed forward-firing: 6 × 20 mm Hispano cannon
Flexible mounted: 6 × 0.303 in (7.7 mm) machine guns
Depth charges: 8 × 250 lb (113 kg)
Anti-submarine equipment
ASV Mk II radar
Crew 7

In November 1943 the Liberator returned to Prestwick for a further overhaul, but by the time the work was complete, the Mark I version had passed out of front-line service in Coastal Command. AM929 was then assigned to No. 231 Squadron based at Dorval in Canada, a transport squadron carrying high priority cargoes and passengers across the Atlantic. The aircraft operated in this role until 9 April 1945 when, following an engine fire, she crashed near Montreal in Canada.

During her 16 months of operations with No. 120 Squadron, those on AM929 sighted U-boats on 25 occasions and converted 14 of those sightings into attacks, which resulted in the sinking of four and the shared destruction of one more. During the 70-odd years

since aircraft first began hunting submarines, no other has come close to the success of Consolidated Liberator AM929. Beyond question, she was the sub-hunting aircraft supreme.

Squadron Leader Terrence Bulloch: Sub-Hunting Pilot Supreme

Born in Lisburn, County Antrim, in 1916, Terry Bulloch joined the Royal Air Force in 1936. After completing his pilot training he joined Coastal Command and flew Ansons, converting to Hudsons soon after the outbreak of war. In November 1940 he was awarded the Distinguished Flying Cross for a series of attacks on enemy shipping. Following this Bulloch went on a "rest" tour and spent the first half of 1941 with Ferry Command flying American-built Fortresses, Liberators, and Hudsons across the Atlantic for delivery to the Royal Air Force.

In the summer of 1941 Bulloch was posted to No. 120 Squadron then forming with Liberator I aircraft modified for maritime patrol operations, and that marked the beginning of his career against submarines. On competing his conversion training he flew the unit's first operational sortie with the new aircraft, an anti-submarine sweep on 20 September which passed off uneventfully. He attacked his first submarine on 22 October, but without inflicting any damage.

In December 1941 Bulloch was promoted to squadron leader, holding official assessments of "Exceptional" as a pilot (the highest grading possible in the RAF) and "Above the Average" as a navigator. He was gifted with exceptional eyesight, was a fine captain who worked hard to form his crew into a well-knit team, and was intensely interested in getting the most out of the ASV radar and the weapons carried by his aircraft. Bulloch's enthusiasm for hunting enemy sub-

marines proved infectious and started to bring results. By the second week in August 1942, his crew had sighted U-boats on seven occasions and attacked three of them, though still without causing serious damage to any. Considering that at this time many Coastal Command crews flew an entire tour of duty time without even seeing an enemy submarine, these figures are remarkable and showed that Bulloch and his men had their share of luck, but they went on to exploit every sighting for almost all it was worth.

Bulloch and his crew inflicted their first serious damage on a U-boat on 16 August 1942, when they attacked *U89* some 500 miles (930 km) off the southwest of Ireland. Two days later the crew repeated the performance against *U653* in a similar area.

As related elsewhere, Bulloch and his crew flew Liberator H-How of No. 120 Squadron when they sank their first submarine, *U597*, on 12 October.

During the three weeks following the sinking of *U597*, Bulloch and his crew sighted four more U-boats and attacked two of them

ASV Mk II radar-fitted Liberator Mk IIIs of No. 120 Squadron in a line at their base, Aldergrove in Northern Ireland on 10 April 1943. The third Liberator from the front is GR Mk Vb equipped with "Dumbo" radar dome under the nose. (Imperial War Museum)

without success. Then, on 5 November, the crew was sent in H-How to support Convoy SC107 which the previous day had lost 15 ships during a concentrated attack from a Wolf Pack of 13 U-boats. As Bulloch arrived in the area, one of his crew sighted a U-boat, but it dived to safety before he could attack it. The lookouts on the next boat sighted, *U132*, were less vigilant, and they paid the supreme price for their laxity; Bulloch surprised her on the surface and laid a stick of depth charges right across the boat which split her hull. Later in the day the crew sighted a third U-boat, which Bulloch attacked with his remaining depth charges but without causing serious damage.

In December 1942 Bulloch and his crew demonstrated just how much a single well-handled aircraft could achieve in the defense of a convoy. Wolf Packs *Draufgänger* and *Panzer* with a total of more than 20 U-boats were closing in to engage eastbound convoy HX217 with 25 merchant ships and five escorts in the area of the Atlantic Gap, and during the early morning darkness on the 8th, a leading boat reached the convoy and torpedoed a merchantman. Then Bulloch and

his crew arrived in the area, and the situation changed immediately. Later the pilot recalled:

"We arrived over the convoy just as it was getting light. We knew there were U-boats around, and we were keeping our eyes skinned. The visibility wasn't too good. There was a sort of half light, and the hail storm didn't improve things. I started my patrol by making a wide sweep round the convoy, and almost at once we struck lucky. Astern of the ships and on the Liberator's port beam, I spotted a submarine traveling fast on the surface. It was going all out to catch the convoy."

During the two hours that followed, the crew attacked three U-boats with depth charges. That expended the Liberator's main weapons, but the aircraft had sufficient fuel to remain in the area, and Bulloch remained on patrol. It was as well that he did because, as the pilot commented, "... the submarines kept bobbing up all over the place. We'd no sooner finished one attack and got all the details logged than another would show up." The German sailors had no way of

The U-boat (Type IXB) under strafing attack by RAF Coastal Command aircraft. (Imperial War Museum)

knowing that their tormentor had only cannon with which to attack them and were forced to dive and lose contact with the convoy. When the Liberator reached the limit of its endurance in the area, another aircraft of No. 120 Squadron arrived to continue the patrol; its crew went on to sight five U-boats and attack four of them.

The two Liberator crews had performed their primary task of safeguarding Convoy HX217 in exemplary fashion and broke up what would otherwise have been a concentrated and overwhelming attack on the merchant ships. The official German Navy account of the action later stated:

"Following an analysis of this action, Flag Officer U-boats stated that the results were poor due to the strength of the escort.."

Certainly it had seemed to the U-boat crews that there had been a lot more than two aircraft patrolling the area round the convoy that day.

Following the action in support of HX217, Bulloch was awarded the Distinguished Service Order, then went on a second "rest" tour to conduct the flight trials of a Liberator fitted with a Leigh Light, and he also tested an air-to-surface rocket installation fitted to the aircraft.

Terrence Bulloch resumed operational flying in the late spring of 1943 and joined No. 224 Squadron flying Liberators. On 8 July he caught *U514* on the surface near Cape Finisterre and launched two devastating attack runs on the boat. During the first pass he fired his eight rockets; then as the boat dived he dropped eight depth charges across her and followed by a "Mark 24 Mine" homing torpedo. There were no survivors from *U514*.

The sinking of *U514* was Bulloch's final success against the U-boats. Altogether he and the crews he commanded sighted enemy submarines on 24 occasions; they attacked 17, three of which were sunk, and two seriously damaged. It was a performance without equal in the long and hard-fought battle between the aircraft and the submarine. Terrence Bulloch ended the war with the DSO and bar, and the DFC and bar.

Attack By A Winning Combination

The sinking of *U597* on 12 October 1942 was the first U-boat kill for Squadron Leader Terrence Bulloch, who would later become the top-scoring anti-submarine pilot, and for Liberator H-How AM929 of No. 120 Squadron, which would later become the top scoring aircraft. Bulloch's tactics on that day were noteworthy. While searching for his prey he held the aircraft just below the cloud base at 2,000 feet (610 m), thus making it as difficult as possible for the U-boat's lookouts to see him coming. And when he dived to attack, he

did so from out of the sun. In this way he was able to surprise *U597* on the surface and release his stick of depth charges accurately down her length from stern to stem. Bulloch's combat report after the action is reproduced below.

U/BOAT ATTACK ASSESSMENT FORM SERIAL No. 260

(a) Date: 12/10/42

(b) Time of attack: 1223 Z hours

(c) Aircraft letter, Squadron and Captain: Liberator I H/120 S/L Bulloch

(d) Relevant CC Form AUB Serial No.: CCAUBV/REY 1.

(e) Details of Report. On passage to convoy ONS 136, flying on track 239° [west-south-west] at 2000 ft, in 7/10ths cloud, base 2000 ft, sea moderate, visibility 15 miles and showery, sighted a wake 50° on starboard bow distant 8 miles. Aircraft turned to starboard to investigate and approached down sun. A U-boat was identified in position 56° 50′ N 28° 05′ W [540 n miles south-south-west of Iceland] course 270° [due west] 10 knots. This position was 46° 15 miles from [westbound Convoy] ONS 136. U-Boat was German 517 ton class, painted greenish-grey color. Aircraft dived to attack from U-Boat's port quarter at 15° to track, releasing from 75′ 6 Mark XI Depth Charges, set to shallow depth, spaced 25′ while U-Boat was still on the surface.

Nos. 6 and 7 Depth Charges failed to release. U-Boat was completely covered by stick both in line and range. Evidence states that No. 1 Depth Charge was right on stern, No. 2 about 35 ft before the stern on the port side, No. 3 and 4 amidships close to the starboard side, 8 right on the bow just on port side. During the explosion of the first depth charge, three large and a number of small pieces of metal were seen to be thrown up into the air; one large oval piece of metal flew past the rear turret just before photograph No. 4405 was taken. As Nos. 3 and 4 Depth Charges were exploding, the U-Boat was seen to shudder with the explosions and lift out of the water, leaving the deck clearly visible with the water pouring off it. As the spray was subsiding, conning tower and one periscope were seen in the middle of the disturbance area. They hung there about 7 seconds and then appeared to sink vertically with no forward movement. After the spray had settled, a white cylindrical object was seen bobbing up and down in the disturbance. Soon after this a patch of oil appeared on the scene of attack and a cylinder, greenish-grey in color, about 5 ft out of the water and a foot or so in diameter, studded with bolts, appeared in this patch of oil and was still floating there when the aircraft left, 27 minutes later. The oil patch was at the leading edge of depth charge explosion mark. R/T was used to inform SNO [senior naval officer] Convoy escorts of the attack and of the wreckage. Message Acknowledged.

A dying U-boat in the Bay of Biscay. (Imperial War Museum)